JUST PLAY

WOODY MANN
STEWART JORDAN

Copyright © 2016 by Woody Mann & Stewart Jordan

All rights reserved.
No reproduction without written permission from the publisher.

First Printing, 2016
Second Printing, 2019

Lee Haywood Studio, Publisher
ISBN-13:978-0692339893

ISBN-10:0692339892

PO Box 903
Times Square Station
New York, NY 10108
acousticsessionsinc@gmail.com

www.woodymann.com

Cover Photograph by Rod Franklin
Cartoon by Justin Green
Book Design by Emily Thompson, Thompson Studio

Contents

Acknowledgments 5

Introduction 7

CHAPTER 1: Getting Started: Rev. Gary Davis,
Yazoo Records and Discovering Mastery 10

CHAPTER 2: Into the Maelstrom: Lennie Tristano 46

CHAPTER 3: Acquiring a Masterpiece 71

CHAPTER 4: Other Orbits: The Zoller System 80

CHAPTER 5: Carlos Paredes: A Mirror of Sounds 96

CHAPTER 6: Just Play 108

CHAPTER 7: How It All Connects 111

CHAPTER 8: And So Play On 125

Notes 127

Further Listening and Resources 134

For my students…

Acknowledgments

This book came about, initially, through the conversations I had with Stewart Jordan driving through the backwaters of the United Kingdom on my 2014 spring tour playing solo guitar shows in regional theaters, clubs and festivals. "Just Play" grew out of those late night talks – and Stewart's willingness to carry on redrafting and editing numerous versions of this manuscript over the last few years.

Thanks to the following people for their contribution to this project: Justine Toye for transcribing and typing up the original interviews in spite of the background noise of many of the interview venues, Dr. Stewart McFarlane, Trevor Laurence, Ianthe Dugan, Terre Roche, Valerie Lettieri Mann, Dana Mann, Ron Buck, Ian Dennis, Nik Munson, Rod Franklin for the cover photo, Emily Thompson for designing the book, and Bronwen Epstein for her editing and proofing.

Introduction

Playing music in the 26th floor stairwell of my apartment building always takes me back to my most important guitar lessons. It is probably because it provides me with a quiet escape from the everyday hassles of living in NYC and provides a sound which reverberates up and down its forty-five floor column of air. The basic "lesson ones" – play slowly, pay attention to each note, feel the time and enjoy the act of making music in that moment. On a good day I can get straight into the music with no negative thoughts or vibes getting in the way to filter the message. It feels effortless. I just play and the stairwell is filled with color and texture. On a bad day I wonder what the hell I'm doing sitting on cold steps with my ass hurting from the concrete...

It's the good days that keep bringing me back to music. I remember at my lessons with the great piano player Lennie Tristano, I would sometimes complain that the music didn't feel good that week, or that I just could not 'connect' with the music. Lennie would ask me:

– *"How much of the many hours you practiced every day felt really good?"*
– *"Well, there was about 10 minutes last Tuesday that felt great!"*
– *"Well, cheer up, you had a good week!"*

There's only one road to getting to that place where the good days outnumber the bad days: staying on course and putting in the time.

I have been lucky enough to have known and worked with a handful of artists who, along the way, became my touchstones – the artists who, when I need it, remind me of my "lesson ones." This book is about them – the musicians Rev. Gary Davis, Lennie Tristano, Attila Zoller, Carlos Paredes, and the guitar makers Jimmy D'Aquisto and John Monteleone. It is about how their artistry informs my music and how I look into their worlds and art through my lens as a student, a friend, and as a musician. I pay homage to them every time I pick up the guitar.

On the face of it, any kind of commonality between the music of Reverend Gary Davis, jazz piano virtuoso Lennie Tristano, jazz guitarist and composer Attila Zoller, the great Portuguese guitar virtuoso Carlos Paredes and the great guitar makers Jimmy D'Aquisto and John Monteleone, is not immediately obvious. Rev. Gary Davis was one of the most inventive blues and ragtime guitar players who ever lived. Even in the 1960's some 30 or 40 years after his hey-day, Davis' playing was more advanced than anyone else working on the scene at that time. The Reverend was my first guitar teacher. I began my lessons at his house in Queens, NY when I was 13 years old. Lennie Tristano came from a completely different world. A contemporary of Charlie Parker, with whom he played frequently during the late 1940s and early 1950s, Lennie managed to develop his own concept of music that he first expressed as a musician in the heart of the New York jazz scene and later as a teacher. I was lucky enough to spend an intensive four-year period of study with Lennie. Some of his many students have achieved recognition in their own right such as Lee Konitz and Warne Marsh. The Hungarian guitarist and composer Attila Zoller was also part of the jazz world, but as a musician who grew up in post-war Europe, he brought a different sensibility and temperament to the music. A true musician's musician, Attila's unique voice has exerted a powerful influence on younger players such as Pat Metheny, a one-time student of Attila's. I met Attila through the NYC music scene and we soon became good friends. His excitement about his music and colorful personality made for some of the most memorable times I've ever had with another musician. From an entirely different European tradition, the Portuguese guitar virtuoso Carlos Paredes was a national hero. His vivid and evocative compositions became a soundtrack to the social history of Portugal in the second half of the twentieth century as that country emerged from decades of brutal dictatorship following the Portuguese Revolution of 1974. And this is not to overlook the music facilitated by the guitar makers Jimmy D'Aquisto and John Monteleone – both New Yorkers of Italian origin who have dedicated their lives to meeting the needs of working musicians and advancing the craft of instrument making. Jimmy and John are the finest guitar makers of their respective times. Period.

I have for some time had an intuitive sense that somehow this admittedly disparate group of artists are connected and not merely by the fact that my path happened to cross theirs. It is easy to say that they shared a certain sensibility, or perhaps more boldly, an authenticity, in their approaches to their craft. It is harder to describe what that sensibility looks and sounds like. But in a nutshell, what connects them is their mastery of their chosen art forms. This is my tribute to their artistry and mastery.

What binds them, at least on one level, is their individual struggle to find a way to live as artists in their immediate surroundings, whether the streets of Harlem, Long Island, or Portugal. To be an artist – to lead a creative life – is difficult. Making a living at it can add other roadblocks. The dilemma is broadly the same as it has always been. The arts do not exist in a vacuum. What connects their personal journeys is their mastery of their chosen art forms.

In hindsight, the time they gave to me was a rare privilege. It is strange to think that something which started with an act as simple as making a telephone call asking for a guitar lesson could lead, decades later, to looking back at such an enriching string of experiences. It all made perfect sense to me at the time. After all, I was a middle class kid growing up in 1960s/70s America and just wanted to play music, make music and above all have fun with it.

Welcome to my music – everyone is invited in.

Chapter 1

Getting Started: Rev. Gary Davis, Yazoo Records and Discovering Mastery

"The term "effortless mastery" is actually redundant because mastery is the effortless execution of music."
Kenny Werner "Effortless Mastery"[1]

I was part of the generation that came of age during the early 1970s. I was a "red diaper" baby. My parents attended political meetings – they were politically engaged and active people. There were meetings and events going on that as a kid I knew little about. Actually, I thought we just had a huge extended family. There were usually about fifty people who turned up at these meetings – my mother told me it was a "cousin club." It was not until I was 18 or so that she told me these meetings were Marxist forums. They were basically book discussions and protest rally organization meetings. Back then, if you were into folk music or involved in the civil rights movement, you were basically branded a communist. In my parent's house we grew up listening to Pete Seeger, Woody Guthrie, Paul Robeson and Leadbelly. These musicians were the heroes in the house. At that time, I was too young to know what a communist was;

I just grew up listening to this amazing music from that time.

I started out playing the clarinet. That was my first instrument. I remember watching television as a kid when Leonard Bernstein hosted a music show for children, which had short films of orchestras and various music ensembles. I saw this instrument, a clarinet, this black thing and thought "That's pretty cool; I like the sound, I'd like to play that." I was seven or eight years old. By the time I got to junior high school, where there were music lessons to be had, I started to play clarinet.

At some point during our childhood, my brothers and sister all took piano lessons – at least for a short time. My mother played a little piano, too. Music was in the house. There was also always a guitar around. My older brother, Mark, played and was into folk music. I really admired my brother. He seemed to have it together: a cool guy, the captain of the wrestling team, popular at school and all that. He showed me some basic chords and strumming and I was hooked. I just dove in and picked it up from any source I could find – from books, trying to imitate the recordings I was listening to at that time – anything that was available to me. There was a Lightning Hopkins[2] LP that was my "go-to" music when I wanted to escape. I was a Big Bill Broonzy[3] fan because his biography was one of my favorite books.[4] I had some old nylon string guitar – my first guitar – but Mark would let me play his steel string guitar, a big dreadnought sized D-18 Martin. It was way too big for me and playing on the steel strings made my fingers hurt like hell – like rubbing the edges of broken glass. But after a while I managed to reach around and get a sound out of the box.

When I was a little older, around fifteen and still in High School, I got into the Julliard Preparatory School. I'd go there usually two times a week. My mother would schedule everything around her picking me up and driving me to the train to go into the city. There I continued to learn the clarinet, studying more of the classical repertoire and getting deeper into formal music studies.

But I still carried on with the guitar away from school. It was two separate tracks; the music school and classical music for clarinet; the guitar for strumming folk music and learning songs such as *Freight Train*, *This Land is Your Land* and *Nobody Knows You When You're Down and Out*. I wasn't conscious of any link between my formal studies at Julliard Prep School and my interest in the guitar. At that time the two certainly didn't join up in my mind. Of course, looking back, the grounding in classical music definitely helped – and shaped – my work on the guitar and other music styles. Blues and jazz just seemed like classical music with a different melody, harmony and rhythm, but otherwise part of the same "toolbox".

In parallel with my classical studies at school my early experiments with coaxing a sound out of my brother's guitar took a fateful twist. It was during the years after the folk music trio Peter, Paul and Mary had a hit with *If I Had My Way*, around 1965, that Reverend Gary Davis[5] was rediscovered on the streets of New York City…

Rev. Davis – A Telephone Call…

I started out playing folk music and from there I discovered the Blues. The recordings of Josh White, Leadbelly, Paul Robeson, Big Bill Broonzy were in my mother's record collection and I just gravitated towards them. It seemed like a logical extension getting into blues music from the folk music repertoire of Pete Seeger and Woody Guthrie, to name a few, that I listened to as I was growing up. I was also listening to players like Dave Van Ronk and was familiar with some of the guitar folk repertoire going around at that time. I had a recording of Peter, Paul and Mary playing *If I Had My Way*, which had been released in 1962 at the start of the folk revival of that decade. I found out that the tune was based on an original song written by Reverend Gary Davis, a name I recognized from the folk guitar tablature books I was learning from. He also wrote *Candyman* and *Cocaine Blues* – two of the anthems of folk guitar playing. At that time I was trying to find a teacher near where I lived, so I just decided to track one down. I knew how to play *Candyman* and thought I would look up Rev. Gary Davis.

To my delight I discovered he lived in Queens, NY only about an hour and a half drive from my home in East Williston, Long Island. I opened the telephone directory and I started to call the numbers listed for 'Gary Davis.' On the third number his wife, Annie Davis, answered the phone. I just asked if this was "the" Gary Davis and, "can I come over?" Annie said, "Sure..." That's how it happened. It was just a telephone call from a kid asking for a guitar lesson. It felt like the most natural thing to do. I didn't realize at the time that this phone call shaped the course of my life. It would open a treasure trove.

I had little knowledge of Davis, no idea of his background, or any particular insight why his music was being covered by a popular folk act of the day. I didn't even know that he was a blind street singer.

When I started taking lessons with Davis I was too young to travel by myself. We lived on Long Island, so my mother would drive me to Davis' house. She would leave me there and go shopping and then return to pick me up, usually about five hours later. She knew folk music but she didn't know his music particularly well. But it was enough for her to know that Davis was an important figure to me. She was my biggest supporter and facilitated it all. I couldn't have traveled to Davis' house on my own at that age – it was my mother who made sure it was safe.

Discovering Davis – The Door to a New Music

I was completely unaware that Davis was probably one of the most important blues, ragtime and gospel guitarists of the twentieth century. I had no idea that he had developed a unique improvisatory approach to playing his music that to this day few musicians have managed to master, let alone surpass. I didn't know his music – only the two tunes I was struggling to get through – *Cocaine Blues* and *Candyman*. I had never heard *Hesitation Blues* or any of the Davis standard tunes. It was a major period of discovery where I also learned about his repertoire. I even remember asking him at my first lesson: "What else do you play?" I simply didn't know what he did. And he said, "You just call for it." I just didn't know what to ask for. So I set about buying his records, getting myself familiar with his tunes and learning what to ask for at my lessons. It's interesting to look back at just how obsessed I became with his guitar playing. For me, even his religious tunes were all about the guitar part. The spiritual lyrics did not resonate with me at that age. I didn't understand his "message". I was just focused on the amazing guitar arrangements and learning that sound.

Unwittingly, it was a first step in taking control and responsibility for my learning. I had to go to his house and ask to learn. I had to call his tunes. Describing this as structuring my own curriculum is perhaps too grand and I certainly didn't think of it in those terms at the time. But in retrospect, that's kind of what happened because with Davis I had to decide what I wanted to play, not what someone else decided to teach me. I had to call the tunes.

Very quickly however, my time with Davis became about more than just guitar lessons. I felt special being there. It was like a musical refuge – a safe place. My father left a few years before I started studying with Davis and the wound was still pretty open. Davis' house was very welcoming and warm. Both he and Annie made me feel good about myself. Davis used to say he was proud to be my teacher. Wow. I would talk about school and what's going on in my life (like he cared) – but he always listened and offered his advice. Sometimes it was odd advice, like the time he told me to bring my school principal around to his house so he could teach him a lesson on how to behave. But he listened, which is more than I could say about my father. As to why Davis chose to give me so much of his time, I don't know. It never occurred to me to ask him.

I just assumed this was how he taught everyone.

The Lessons – Finding a "Center"

There was no methodology to Davis's lessons. You just played it like him – pure imitation. The lessons were about going back and forth over the material. They were actually just very repetitive. And it was slow. Drill, drill, drill and more drill. After two or three hours of that, my hands would be dropping off. But he wouldn't let me leave his house until I had learned it. The process was largely about constant correction, back and forth, one song after another. He wouldn't move me on until I had got it. Then we would jam on it endlessly. It was just exciting for me to hear (and see) how he could improvise so naturally.

What strikes me most about Davis as a teacher was his patience. It was as if he had nothing better to do than to play the guitar. Davis was devoted to his music, and as a teacher he was equally devoted to teaching his music to his students.

He didn't have a dedicated teaching room or anything like that. The front door opened into the living room, and that is where he would teach. That's where he spent most of the day. His easy chair was right next to the front door and I would be sitting in front of him so we were constantly being interrupted. Annie, his wife, would be cooking in the kitchen, church folks would be coming and going, kids running around – somehow we never seemed to mind. Many times Davis' gardener and family friend, Moses, would be mowing the lawn and singing along to whatever tune we were playing. The lessons took place in a very natural environment – they were just part of everyday life in the Davis household. And gradually, as I got to know the Reverend and Annie better, I think that I became part of that ebb and flow of family life. It is just the way they were as people, very open and warm. It was, at least to me, a very safe environment.

I remember during one of my first visits he said to me, "Empty my bucket, boy," and pointed to a can hidden under his big easy chair. It was a coffee can with a little water in it. He used it as an ashtray so he could "hear" the ashes go out when they hit the water. He would also use it for other choice 'waste products.' At the start of one particular lesson he just sat there and said, "Empty my bucket, boy." So I thought it was some rite of passage. Two days worth of coffee dregs, piss and cigar ash. "Empty my bucket and put it back," he said. It was disgusting – trying to tip it all down the toilet without coming into contact with it. I was very proud of myself. The cigar ash was a constant problem though. He would sit there smoking and the column of ash at the end of the cigar would get longer and longer. And you would try and catch the ash before it fell onto the guitar – the ash was hot and would burn his guitar. In fact, there was a hole in the guitar he was using at that time which obviously fitted perfectly with the hot ash dropping off his cigars.

I think Davis was proud of me – as his student. I recall him one time, "Come in here Annie, what do you think?" And she replied, "Sounds like you Brother Davis." And that was really like a seal of approval. I knew that he liked the way I played his songs. I think he dug my playing.

For me, Davis' house was the focus. This was the place where I learned with him. It was my safe haven. I didn't know him when he was playing music on the streets or living in condemned buildings in the Bronx. I met him at a time in his life when he had a modicum of success and was living comfortably in his house in Jamaica, Queens. I was too young at that stage to drive him around or go out on the road or to gigs like some of his older students. So I didn't know first-hand about the incidents with the guns or any of the other secular stories. I was just a kid who took lessons with him at his house. I was so proud to be studying with him and felt like I discovered a part of myself. I wanted my friends to hear Davis' so I put on a house concert for Davis in my living room. I remember printing the tickets. My mother and sister made brownies and coffee. It was nice that we made about $350 for him, which was a fair amount in those days. He just asked me not to tell his manager. There was a dramatic twist to the occasion though. As between fifty and one hundred High School kids were waiting for the concert to begin, Davis was sat in a comfy chair snoring his head off. The Reverend was out cold. Evidently the "greasers" (the older kids who could drive and buy alcohol) had come in and had given him booze beforehand. I didn't understand what Davis meant when he asked for his "medicine." But they did. I managed to wake him when I put on one of his records and turned an amplifier up to maximum – he got up like a shot. Aside from this occasion and going to his church a few times, my contact with Davis was pretty much exclusively at his house in Jamaica, Queens. But I was getting to know him better as a person and would hang out, sometimes for hours after the lesson, waiting for my mother to pick me up. Once he was telling me a story about "exercising your hips" and how to treat women. I had no idea what he was talking about. Instead, I'd ask him to play a blues, knowing that it was not allowed in the house. Annie only allowed gospel, ragtime and pop tunes in the house – but no blues. Blues was the devil's music and this was a church house. But I'd keep asking and every now and then he would launch into *Cross and Evil Women Blues,* one of the few tunes he played in the key of E. He never discussed the blues or talked about blues artists. Blues was something he played in his early days, before he was ordained as a Minister. Aside from the lyrics, it was a fine line between gospel and blues. What is too bluesy a guitar part for church? I still have not figured that one out.

I think that one of the lessons from the hours I spent at Rev. Davis' house is putting music at the center of your life. I loved the fact that at the lessons, music was part of whatever was happening in the house. Just put your instrument(s) into your living room and allow making music to become part of your everyday life, your habit, or whatever. Why shut it away in a "music room"? Davis would sit in his front room and just hold court there. The music, the teaching – it was at the core of who he was.

In addition to my all day guitar lessons in Reverend Davis' front room I was becoming immersed in the blues music scene through traveling to the various folk and blues festivals springing up at that time. When I was about 15 years old I made it to a blues festival in Michigan. There I met Nick Perls, who owned one of the best 78 record collections of classic blues around. I was about to get even deeper into blues music – total intoxication with no known cure.

Blues Lessons at Nick Perls' House:
Revivalists, Record Collectors and Record Labels

In the life of anyone who can be said to have mastered anything there is a period where they do that thing to the exclusion of almost everything else. Perhaps you can describe it as tunnel vision, devotion, stubbornness, mania, even perhaps selfishness. Maybe it is something comprised of all of these traits. For me, in addition to my lessons with Rev. Gary Davis, my immersion in Blues music deepened even further when I fell in with a group of New York based enthusiasts and supporters of American roots music, all linked in some way to a small, independent record label, Yazoo Records.

An important influence was the scene that Nick Perls created in New York during the 1960s and 1970s. That scene gave me an overview of the whole of American "roots" music in which I mean all American musical forms and styles, including ragtime, Appalachian mountain music, blues, bluegrass, folk and early jazz music. I gained access to all sorts of music at an early age which opened my ears to a range of diverse influences. I also met the people involved in that scene including Nick, Steve Calt, John Fahey and Mike Stewart who exerted a long-reaching influence on me in terms of thinking about music and placing in terms of social and historical contexts. Above all, I learned how to evaluate the music for myself, to question the assumptions made by others. Through the conversations, discussions and arguments I had during that time, I developed my own point of view.

For me Nick was a patron of the arts. I first met him at a blues festival in Michigan when I was about 15 years old. He heard me play a few Blind Blake[6] tunes and asked me if I'd like to come over to his place in New York City the following week to check out his collection of blues 78s. Once I saw his collection I was hooked. It was housed along a thirty-foot wall of his basement. The wall was lined with rows of 78s, each in an archival light green cover. There must have been thousands, A to Z starting with Texas Alexander. I used to spend the whole day at Nick's place listening to 78s while he did his work. He let me handle the discs and showed me how to play them on his old antique record player with all the noise reduction equipment so I could transfer them to tape. I had dozens of reel-to-reel tapes of rare recordings. I still have boxes of them today. Very quickly my world revolved around Nick's place. He opened his house to me and supported my music as well. He also respected my ideas about blues music. I really felt like I had something to offer. Nick was inspirational in that way – a key figure in fanning the flames of my burgeoning enthusiasm for the music.

Nick Perls was also a key individual in raising public awareness of "country blues" music. He was instrumental in putting a huge number of important records into the public domain, primarily through his Yazoo Record label. His stockpile of 78s was one of the largest collections in the world made up of records released under old labels such as Paramount, Victor, Vocalion, Columbia. He reissued a great number of them as anthology albums on his own label. His father was an art-importer so Nick was well off. He lived in a fancy house in Greenwich Village, which of course, the record label didn't pay. Country blues albums were not exactly big sellers. Yazoo was basically a vanity label. But it was an important one.

The role of Yazoo Records was significant in terms of preserving country blues the music and making it available to a wider audience (or at least wider than the dozen or so collectors of the old 78 disks who were around at that time). But you have to remember that it was a small-scale, niche record label. To give you a sense of the scale of the operation, back in the late 1960s or early 1970s, if a Yazoo record sold three hundred copies, it was considered to be a big seller. It was a very specialized market, which is why Nick ran the label (together with its sister label, Blue Goose Records, that specialized in contemporary blues artists) as a hobby. The record covers and the artwork were all done "in-house." There was little budget.

The label was essentially a one-man business. To survive, it relied on Nick's personal wealth and the contributions (although he paid them) of enthusiasts and supporters, from the art work by Robert Crumb to the liner notes drafted by Steve Calt, Don Kent, and others. So the whole blues scene was very small. Nick would project manage the whole production process for each record release, from capturing the sound of his scratchy old 78s onto new vinyl, to selecting the photos (or using Robert Crumb's artwork) for the album sleeve. Usually Steve Calt or one of the other record collectors wrote the liner notes to each new release. Generally, Steve was Nick's "go-to" guy when it came to key decisions about the direction of each record project.

Nick's house became the hub for all sorts of activity: record collectors would have parties and trade music; historians would gather to discuss records. Anybody who came through New York, any blues artist, would stay at Nick's house or he would sponsor them. He put on countless lunches and dinners – he used to call me up and say, "Fahey's in town," or, "Son House is in town," or Hacksaw Harney. At that time I was living on 10th Street and I would be over to Nick's place in a shot. After hanging and playing records or jamming we would all go out to dinner, sometimes it would be a big crowd, maybe 10 people or more. We would have a great meal and Nick would always pick up the tab. I was younger than the others, so I tended to be more of a fly on the wall at these dinners – I didn't have the knowledge of the history of the music to join in fully, nor did I have a huge collection of 78s to talk about. This was except for the occasions when we talked about what key a particular tune was in – then I could contribute.

I met so many people who were involved with the small folk/blues scene in NY. I remember coming back from dinner one night and running into a bunch of people I knew. They headed back to Nick's place (I think because he always had the best marijuana in town). I remember Phil Ochs and Jack Elliott were there, together with a host of other folk musicians and Greenwich Village regulars. But I remember being totally star-struck. I had all of their albums. Through Nick, I also met Jo Ann Kelly and Larry Johnson, two of the greatest contemporary blues artists (but very different people.) The folk and blues scenes were pretty much the same back then. It was a much more connected world of music and people.

Nick's basement was also the place I first recorded. That session I was so nervous that I couldn't sing. Larry was in the room so he sang and I just backed him up on the guitar. Meeting Hacksaw Harney was exciting because he recorded in the 1920s with his brother as "Pet and Can" backing up Lottie Beaman. It was a real discovery. And man could he play. He was totally together, clean, fast, and inventive. I loved listening to him. He also turned out to be a pleasant human being, which frequently wasn't always the case when I met my heroes.

Bill Williams was another musician who I met through Nick. He said he knew Blind Blake and he played a lot of ragtime tunes. He was also a sweetheart. When I was in college in Ohio (in the space between my time at Juilliard School and starting at New York University, I spent a year at Wilmington College, Ohio), Nick called and said someone sent him a tape of an old blues guy who lived in Greenup Kentucky and sounded like Blind Blake. The town was a few hours from my School and Nick asked me to check out this lead. It wasn't easy. I drove down with a friend to Greenup Kentucky, a hard place to find even on a county map. We had no address, just the town. We figured how hard could it be to track down a guitar player in his 70s (or 80s) who had lived in the same small town his entire life. The main street was a quarter mile. We checked the post office, the sheriff's department, the local diner... nothing. Nobody had heard of Bill Williams. After a few hours we were about to leave town when I pulled over to a guy mowing his lawn and asked if he ever heard of Bill: "Nope". For some reason I said "Bill Williams, the guitar player, a black guy?" Almost immediately he said, "Oh you mean Nigger Bill?" He pointed, "Yeah, right there, past the trees, third shack to the left." Bill William's little house was literally on the "other side of the tracks." We drove through the trees that obscured the railroad tracks that ran through town and sure enough, found the "other" Greenup, unpaved streets of rows of houses (shacks) with kids playing in the streets, activity all around. In this Greenup everybody knew Bill, the guitar player. We made it to his house and he welcomed us in. In about 5 minutes, it seemed, the whole shantytown was crowding his living room. He was famous for his 'tomato wine' and we sat and had a glass. I tried to enjoy it and drink the whole thing. Soon, the sheriff came by and asked if "we boys were all right." He didn't understand why two white kids were here. I think he was looking out for us. Anyway, we spent the day playing music together and listening to Bill's incredible music. He said he knew Blind Blake... the stories, the rags, the tomato wine... I was in heaven.

Nick invited Bill to New York and the three of us spent a lot of time together and recorded extensively when we got enough material down. Nick would record everything in those sessions at his house. He captured a lot of good music on those home tapes. It was always a special occasion when Mike Stewart, known professionally as "Backwards Sam Firk," was in town. Mike was an amazing guitarist (he passed away prematurely on October 11, 2007, at the age of 67). He was like an encyclopedia of the blues and the only person that captured the nuance and sound of the old guys. He was THE guitarist who was into country blues at the time. He would play it all – from Bo Weavil Jackson[7] and Little Hat Jones[8] through to John Hurt. But the revelation to me was that he didn't just play through a set of arrangements – he was playing the 'texture' of the music and really got into the nuance of that aspect of blues music. He nailed it. It was a total thrill to hear this guy play. That's when I realized that playing 'country blues' is all about the sound. I would play the same tunes as Mike, but at that time he had been playing blues music for a lot longer than I had, so he got way deeper. I loved listening to him.

Some crazy characters and some great musicians floated through Nick's place in those days. And with both of Nick's labels in full buzz – Yazoo for the re-issues of the old 78's and Blue Goose for the contemporary players – the scene was busy. I met John Fahey at Nick's place. When John was in town he became part of the dinner crowd. At those dinners John would usually hold court and there would be heated conversations about why Skip James[9] used open D minor tuning, or the meaning of Henry Thomas' tunes.[10] I think John liked my playing and he asked me to back him up on a few gigs and record his next album with him. John shared Steve Calt's non-romantic view of the 'country blues' – and because of his research and knowledge, his comments were always thought provoking, insightful and challenging. There was a respect of the music and the artists, which under-pinned his unrelenting cynicism and snide judgments of other historians.

I was over the moon when John asked me to record with him. We rehearsed and arranged an eclectic mix of tunes – a turn of the century show tune, an Indian chant, a blues, and few of his instrumental excursions into never-never land. After I recorded the album with John, he wanted to produce my solo record for his own record label, Takoma Records. I learned a lot being in the studio with him. We recorded my album it but it was never released because of a management shakeup at Takoma records. Let's leave it at that.

I wasn't a 78 record trader – I couldn't have afforded the outlay of acquiring the original 78s on pocket money alone. But Nick kind of took me under his wing. I devoured his record collection.

I think Nick liked me around because I could play the music. The collectors would sit around and they would discuss Blind Blake, Blind Lemon Jefferson[11] or Charlie Patton[12] etc... and they would ask, "Woody, what key is this song in?" and I would reply, "Oh, it's in the key of C." So I found a niche within that group as 'the musical guy.' At that point I didn't know anything about the history of the music, the long-defunct record labels, the obscure artists, but I could figure out the music. They would just ask, "Hey Woody, is this an open G or an E?" and I'd go "No, open D. Low-grade stuff, OK." It was great fun.

The conversations at these meetings were fascinating to me. For example, it could start with Nick and the group deciding, "Let's put out a Big Bill Broonzy record." And they would go around the room: "What are your top fifteen Broonzy songs?" The group would then spend a whole afternoon discussing which are his best pieces and which ones should be on the LP record. It was a lot of fun for me, and that's how I learned to get tunes off records, by really listening to the songs. We would listen to hundreds, maybe thousands, of records. We would listen to anything, all kinds of music. And we would analyze the music: "Where is it from"; "What do you think of this?" And I would love the challenge of being asked, "What key is this tune in?" Even today I just love that – because I'm always right! I love the challenge of being stumped and then trying to figure it out. There are a few records I can think of over the years that stumped me, that took me a long time to decipher. Some of Blind Lemon Jefferson's stuff was tricky, a couple of Blind Blake tunes too. I just loved doing it; I don't know why, it's just a funny thing.

The musicians that Nick, Steve and those guys really went for were the more kinetic players – Charlie Patton, Bo Weavil Jackson, Son House and the like. But as far as the finger-pickers such as Blind Blake and Reverend Gary Davis were concerned, they were not their favorites. It was like, "That's Woody's thing, he's into that." I liked the other guys too, but I was partial Davis and all the ragtime players. They put out the Davis record ("The Complete Early Gary Davis" – Yazoo 2011) and a few other things, so they knew of his importance, but I don't think he was their favorite. They liked the blues that were more musically raw, spontaneous in your face, in the moment, totally unique and spontaneous. Wild. And that's why they were popular; people respond to their excitement and dynamism. Whereas, for example, Mississippi John Hurt wasn't particularly exciting in the same way. He was a good picker, but not an incendiary performer. The same, in my opinion goes for Frank Stokes and Bo Carter[13]. They were great in their own way, but they didn't have the same immediacy as a Charlie Patton. The other players, Big Bill Broonzy, Reverend Gary Davis, Bo Carter, Frank Stokes, were all great of course but not quite the same. Someone like Bo Weavil Jackson or Big Joe Williams were really rough-edged. They are playing pure percussion and unstructured free vocal lines, as intense but even more raw than the elegance of Charlie Patton. But back then (like now) people just responded to it on an emotional, visceral level. I mean it's hard not be moved by the frantic playing and singing of Bo Weavil or Big Joe Williams – it's just so direct, calm in a way, in the moment.

As a music-obsessed teenager, I kind of dug the pre-occupation with the blues tradition within the Yazoo record set, even though I was hanging out with people much older than myself. It was during one of these meetings that I first met Steve Calt. He, more than anyone else around that group, became for me a crucial sounding board for new ideas and perspectives on blues, ragtime and folk music. American Roots. He was the first person who placed the music into a social and historical context that made any sense to me.

How to Approach the Histories (with a pinch of salt):
Steve Calt – A Personal Evaluation

It is necessary to devote time to honing your craft, but part of that process is the need to develop the ability to critique the work of others, as well as your own. In short, you need to learn how to discriminate – to filter what you need to know out from the white noise. Steve showed me, by his example, the importance of developing your own point of view, of working out your own position on a subject by thinking it through to the point where you can say, "This is what I stand for; this is what my music is about." He set out the context and framework to the music, and gave me first insights as to why the artists who created blues music developed their music like they did.

I knew Steve as a writer, a researcher, an enthusiast, and above all as a friend. Later on, we also collaborated on the music, some of the fruits of which were our collaborations on songs like "Cheap Cherry Wine", "East Side Story", "God Works in Mysterious Ways". I loved the way Steve played guitar and wrote songs. Steve was very spontaneous and had this "Charlie Patton" way of playing; off the cuff, very rhythmic and eccentric, based on the old records, but totally original with very sharp lyrics. He recorded a record for Nick, on the Blue Goose label, with the singer Dave Mann (no relation). Nick knew it wouldn't sell, but he put out the record anyway. His tunes were completely original – both his music and his lyrics were creative and contemporary. To me they captured what the country blues is all about. It was exciting to listen to, and it was a great adventure to play with Steve.

We didn't hit it off immediately. In fact when I first met him, at Nick's house, he wouldn't even to talk to me. He had some kind of chip on his shoulder. To him, I was just another kid guitar player passing through, so why should he make the effort. For months he totally dissed me, and then finally one night we were sitting on the couch and he turned to me and said, "Who do you listen to? Who do you like?" I went down a list of people, and happened to mention Bo Weavil Jackson. As soon as I mentioned Jackson he said, "Bo Weavil, no kidding, me too. Hi, I'm Steve Calt". We must have talked for a hour and became immediate friends. It was just because I mentioned Bo Weavil Jackson. That's kind of how nutty he was.

Steve and Nick had this big, stormy relationship, and Steve had a lot of problems getting along with many people, but somehow we got along great. I was younger so I guess I wasn't a big threat to him in terms of competing as a writer or anything. We would hang out in coffee shops and talk all night long. I just dug the eccentricity of it. He would call me up and ask me about a certain artist or style and we'd be off. If I was writing a transcription book, for example the "Anthology of Blues Guitar," I would call him up and he would help me with writing the notes to the music. I guess we complemented each other. I could pick and transcribe the music; he would carry out the historical research and write up the notes. I think he valued and appreciated my perspective on the music. Steve was a huge part of my life and my education.

For me, Steve was the guy who really understood the history of blues music. Almost uniquely for a writer, he also understood the musicians. We would endlessly discuss how the music developed and why the artists played in the way that they played. I always describe him as a real "newspaper guy." His books reflected that side of him. He backed up what he was saying with facts. And he challenged you to back up your views with supporting evidence. I have always found it a curious thing that for the most part people are not really interested in the facts about the blues. They prefer the story and the romance of the music. The historians and record collectors I was aware of also viewed the blues through a romantic eye. Steve tried to figure out the development of the music based on the real history and events. As a result, I think Steve's work was an invaluable contribution to the music and elevated the country blues and early African American traditions to a historically legitimate level. His thesis was that blues is an art form and not a simple 'black folk' music.

Steve's non-romanticised view of the music as an art form and craft is borne out in my experience and supported by the example of Rev. Gary Davis' musicianship and unique approach to playing the guitar. Although Steve was lukewarm towards Davis' music, he understood it in terms of the depth of craft and his originality.

Steve recognized in Davis a master musician within the ragtime and blues idiom.

Sadly I lost touch with Steve towards the end of his life. As he got older he became more eccentric. Every inch of his apartment was filled with boxes of books and newspapers and he would sit typing away, smoking cigarettes, drinking coffee, frantically writing his latest manuscript. There was always a new take on the Kennedy assassination or a new angle on Christianity, Jesus or Charlie Patton. I tried to contact him but he was evicted from his apartment and disappeared. He just ended up on the street and his eccentricity turned in to a kind of paranoia, deeper and deeper. He called me a few times from a pay phone and left a voice message in a weird, strained, mumbled voice, "Hey Woody, I'm on the street with no money, hmm," but he never left a number or contact point.

Rev. Gary Davis – Music as a Craft

If you asked me to describe Davis's approach to the guitar and his music in as few words as possible, I would say that it was immediate and very tactile. It was all about the sound. That's all. He just sat there and pulled this big, rich sound out of the box. Although he had his own style, his "sound," the range of sounds he could get out of the guitar – his palette if you like – was diverse. He could be a very subtle player in that way.

In terms of his approach to his playing, I don't think Davis conceptualized it in terms of "improvisation" as we tend to think of it these days. At my lessons, I remember trying to work out his tunes as set compositions – right down to the last note. Then I would go to my next lesson and he would always play the tune with a different twist, or incorporate an entire new phrase within the song, or a different variation of the main theme or riff. This drove me crazy until I realized he was teaching me his entire approach to playing, not just a collection of songs. He was improvising…

To him it was all part of the same bag. So, even the variations he spun on a tune, what we might call improvisation, were to him just part of the same set piece. And the reason for this is that to Davis, syncopation (the ability to change the emphasis of the music by stressing different notes, beats or accents in the music – like a rhythmic form of counterpoint) was just the normal way of playing. Syncopation was not improvising to Davis, it was just part of the tune. It was about the subtleties of making changes of emphasis while playing on a set theme.

When describing Davis' approach to syncopation, the best place to start is with Davis' words, as he once said during one of my lessons:

"You know... you have the quarter notes and half notes... you figure that out, you understand. But then you have to give it a beat – some kind of rhythm – because, you know, that's the whole thing... Now a melody, yeah – that can be trouble."

This is slightly homespun, but Davis' meaning is clear enough – his words encapsulate the approach. Even though the chords, riffs and melodies may be unique to each tune, there is a common idea to his playing approach – and in time you can start to see the connection between all of Davis' tunes. His finger-picking style is basically a two-line idea. Similar to the two handed approach of the piano. The bass line is played with the thumb of the picking hand driving the rhythm, groove and the underlying feel of his music. The treble line is played with the fingers, usually on the top (higher) strings of the guitar. When you were learning with Davis, the main goal was to achieve independence of rhythm and sound between these two lines – the bass line and the treble. The greater the degree of independence between these two lines – the bass line played with the thumb and the melody line played with the fingers – the easier it becomes to negotiate the syncopation – and capture the nuances of the music. It is this basic, contra-punctual, picking idea, that is the foundation of Gary Davis' approach.[14] This is opposed to the organized "pattern pick" approach you find with almost anything by Merle

Travis, Doc Watson or Chet Atkins, for example. These are different traditions both using a two line approach to finger-style guitar technique – they are just very different.

To build up your own technique on the guitar, to get to the point where you are able to play this way, it is a good idea to play songs slowly with just the base line to get the feel, then add the treble line on top. In learning traditional and country blues guitar it is best to start with songs that are less syncopated and in which the bass line falls on the beat (such as Mississippi John Hurt's *Ain't No Tellin'* or Mance Libscomb's *Sugar Babe*). Then once you have developed a feel for these relatively simple styles, you will find it easier to pick up and master tunes where the picking is less organized, such as Blind Lemon Jefferson, Scrapper Blackwell or Charlie Patton, for example;[15] or even Gary Davis. It really is that process of breaking the music down to it's essence; the bass line and the melody line.

The Building Blocks – Davis's Repertoire

I have come to realize that, basically, Davis had his bag of songs, and that each was a set arrangement. It was a recent revelation to me while making the documentary on Davis' life and music "Harlem Street Singer" that he recorded the same tunes 30 years apart. If you listen to the Yazoo Records release of Davis' 1935 sessions and then compare the recordings of, say, *I Belong to the Band, I Am the Light of This World* or *Banks of The River,* all re-recorded approximately 30 years later in the early 1960s, the arrangements are essentially the same.

It is clear that Davis had his songs worked out. He had his "toolbox" of riffs and ideas, but he was also following a script. At the time of my lessons, I thought that his playing was completely spontaneous and off the wall. But that was because I hadn't at that stage worked out the arrangement aspects of his songs. He spun further improvisations on his tunes and riffs by playing around with the syncopation, emphasizing either the bass line or the treble line, rather like a recording engineer playing with the faders on his or her recording desk. Davis would emphasize one line or the other, play hard or soft, play the arrangement simply or perhaps become more embellished with each chorus.

Basically, you start by learning the tunes. Just learn a handful of short, relatively straightforward tunes – by rote. That way you build up your basic repertoire – your "bag." Then, after a while you start to connect the songs. For example, look at Robert Johnson's tunes in the key of A in standard tuning, for example, *Kind Hearted Woman, Me and the Devil*. Or listen to his tunes in open G tuning – *Terraplane Blues* or *Stop Breakin' Down* – you will hear that they are cut from the same mould in terms of their structure and even their basic riff. So, you can start to "cut and paste" the different parts of the tunes, for example, take the first four bars phrase of *Kindhearted Woman*, add it to the next two bars of *Me and the Devil*, then maybe take the solo from Phonograph Blues – and you have spun another variation on the same theme. My experience was that I became more flexible in what I could play over a 12 bar blues in the key of A by becoming so familiar with all of the riffs that I knew in that key that they became instinctive. I think that the same concept applies to other styles of music such as jazz.

The thing about Davis is that he was really just so good at this. So his blues, rags, gospel tunes used a lot of the same material and the same approach. He was playing, essentially, the same tunes. And so the lesson here is that if you really know your shit, you can improvise. You can take a simple tune, and if you really know it, you can start to play around with it and generate new variations on that tune – all within the same form. And this way, you never get bored with playing the same tunes.

Rev. Davis:

"You play just what you know... that's all you can do. Then, you understand,

its all quiet when you go up against anybody... just play what you know. You go out in the world and say what you got to say... that's all."

Davis' music is a great introduction into the idea of improvisation. He didn't even call it improvisation - it was part of the tune. It is accessible and, with a little time and effort, is it user-friendly. Once students have the hang of it, in my experience most of them don't go back to "pattern playing" – most of them are unable to do so because they have opened up their ear to an inspiring and creative way of making music. And once you have absorbed that lesson, there is no going back. Your music will be in a different place.

Where Does Davis' Music Come From?
(And Why He is an Important Musician)

The southern musicians developed their style out of their experiences. Davis was no different – his music reflected his circumstances. He was a blind street musician who was also a Baptist Minister. His repertoire ranged from novelty tunes, folk songs, pop tunes and gospel tunes. When he played in his church, he figured out a way to play the melody of a gospel tune with chords (basically, a simple form of chord melody) and developed a way of playing that nobody else did. He added this to his blues background to create that beautiful mixture of techniques and repertoire, which is instantly identifiable as Davis' sound.

For me another thing that sets Davis apart, is the way in which his melody lines and improvisations play off the underlying harmony or even a simple bass line. I suspect that his style, in part at least, developed out of the gospel tradition that he was brought up in.

I have often wondered who played gospel music in that harmonic sphere of Davis? The only answer I have ever come up with is "nobody that I can think of." There isn't really a "school" of playing that way. In general, the gospel tunes are a little more melodic and more of a harmonic rhythm than the familiar 12-bar blues structure. You hear this approach in piano-based gospel music (for example, Georgia Tom Dorsey or even Little Brother Montgomery), but on the guitar there is no one else I can think of who was doing anything similar to Davis. Maybe this is why he is a footnote in the history books. People don't quite know what to make of him because he is not a jazz player, he is not a blues player, he is not viewed as a folk singer. Since no one played like him, he doesn't represent a "tradition," a movement, or a "school." Davis' music just happens to fall between these artificial categories.

Categories – Stones in Your Pathway to Mastery

Historians and writers love to carve the musical landscape of America into categories. This obsession with classifying music ultimately detracts from our understanding of the music. That exercise does nothing to inform or enhance it. In fact, the whole debate about "which music belongs where" completely misses the point. It isn't about learning this style or that style, about following this "school" of music or that particular "region" of music. It is about the individual artists and finding your own voice – and Davis certainly had his own voice.

As a player and student, the fixation with putting music into categories can narrow your scope and restricts your ideas. It is a distraction from the real objective, focusing on the craft of your music, the essence of the individual, and what makes you a compelling artist. The problem I have with the ethno-musicologists categorizing music is that it can get in the way of musicians learning music.

With Davis, it wasn't about learning a style, or a set of mannerisms, which you could call blues, ragtime or whatever. Although he would not have articulated it in these terms, it was more like, "Here is your melody, here are your triads, and here are your chords. No licks, no hip endings. Just play that and it will come together."

"Blues Literature" – A (Brief) Personal Opinion (or The Curse of Categories)

In my view blues and folk music are not particularly well served by the literature. The value of a piece of writing about music is whether it helps to demystify or add to our understanding of the 'craft' of the music – about how certain musicians achieved 'mastery'. Many of the books written about blues music show how easy it is to get distracted from the essential message – that the genre is defined by the individual musicians, and that their journeys to master their chosen art form is what the history is all about.

On the positive side, field researchers such as Alan Lomax, Samuel Charters and Mack McCormick did at least take blues music seriously at a time when few others did. As to whether the artists they re-discovered in the 1960s would have re-emerged and gained a wider exposure without their patronage, we will never know for sure. My hunch is that the folk music revival of the 1960s would probably have happened anyway – maybe not in quite the same way, but probably yes. There was a wider interest in roots, blues and folk music at that time, and I am sure that this music would have found an outlet. There was a public appetite to hear the "old-time" music.

Did these writers confer certain legitimacy on the music? Probably yes. For example, Alan Lomax's work for the Library of Congress did offer a prestige on roots music that certainly hadn't existed prior to his appointment as Assistant in Charge of the Archive of Folk Song of the Library of Congress.[16] But in the process, what has happened is that the man himself has been elevated to a position of such prestige basically as a result of one person becoming the purveyor of taste in all matters of roots music.

I wonder whether the question of whether someone else thinks that the music is or is not legitimate is really that important? For example, some of the early commentaries on the blues contained little or no coverage of Charlie Patton, Son House or Skip James.

Although their recordings were rare, dedicated field researchers and collectors of the old 78" records would surely have known them. Now, these look like glaring omissions for these musicians are now widely recognized as three of our most important blues musicians. Why were these figures, initially at least, omitted from the canon by those considered to be "experts"? Further, these writers had no interest in removing the idea of hierarchy, the idea that some art forms are higher than others, from the field cultural/ethno-musical study. They merely re-ordered the hierarchy, putting their own preferences at the top of the pile. Basically, they excluded artists and art forms that they didn't value or did not fit into the categories they created.

I applaud those writers who were starting to think about the links between music and social issues, in particular the issues of gender equality and race equality. They did try to relate the music to current issues, which were then (and still are) hugely important, such as civil rights. There was at least some sense of trying to place the music into its social context.

But in spite of these positive aspects to their work, it is difficult to get beyond their self-interest, and the sense that many of these writers seem to have shared that they somehow owned the music. Almost without exception, these writers were very territorial about who was in and who was out of the canon. I often get the sense that they mistook their discoveries as somehow being more important than the music itself – the creative act or craft of the music. In their advocacy for the music, they somewhere along the line acquired a sense that it was "their" music – theirs to decide whose music counted and whose music was marginalized.

The "story" became the story of their rediscoveries – the thrill and prestige of tracking down an aging "bluesman" and presenting their quarry to a predominately college-kid audience. The lives of the musicians were re-imagined to serve the agendas and pre-occupations of the historians rather than their desire to document the musicians lives in terms which they themselves would have recognized.

For example, while it is true that Lomax championed many artists, most notably Leadbelly, when you read *The Land Where The Blues Began,* above all else, Lomax champions himself. Lomax's account of his own quest is given priority to those who actually created and performed the music.

This is not to belittle the research he carried out. It was important to document as much of the music as possible to preserve it for future generations. But I would have preferred to see it documented in a way which gave primacy to the main subject matter, that of the music rather than the story of its author. As writing, it would have been a more powerful statement had he done so.

On balance, these writers played a number of positive roles. But is has to be remembered that none of them actually wrote or created the music. They were authors, but they were never "The Authors".

Most of what has been written about the blues could have been improved if the authors had removed the romantic lens through which they imagined that the music occurred. Tracing the musicians through their influences, would have resulted in a different 'history' of the music and a more accurate one in my view. Even the term "country blues" is not defined. Writers do not attempt to "explain the characteristics of 'country blues' but merely brandish the term as a superlative."[17] Where does the term 'country blues' come from? Steve Calt identified its first usage in the liner notes to the 1957 Folkways release "Big Bill Broonzy Sings Country Blues" prepared by Charles Edwards Smith. The basic problem with the term "country blues" is that, as Steve succinctly noted: "there was nothing to support the notion of blues as a music of any particular origin, rural or urban. Its history was simply invented by writers."[18] The researchers, the historians, the ethnomusicologist, the record collectors did not really succeed in making sense or order out of the "field" of early blues music. The very act of trying to impose an order or was misplaced. For example, the use of geography as a basis for analyzing and categorizing the music does not stack up.

It's too simplistic to carve-up of the musical landscape in terms of where it came from geographically, i.e. the primitive sounds of Alabama, the ragtime sounds of the Carolina's, the more sophisticated approaches of the musicians from St. Louis. Also, for many blues writers, it would seem that folk music could not come from the city.

It is an easy trap to group the musicians and assign a certain technique or musical definition to a regional territory. These boundaries, mostly created by historian's speculations, can be misleading. Like any musical tradition, the blues can sometimes be a bewildering and wonderfully confusing music that rarely conforms to a definition. The recordings themselves do not necessarily represent the complete picture of the music at the time. How many gifted musicians went unrecorded we will never know. In addition, it is difficult to view the music outside the environment in which it was played. Whatever was required for a playing situation – be it dances, the streets, church, or the clubs – was probably the main factor in developing an individual style or sound.

In some areas there was one guitarist who was so influential and popular that many other players copied his style. These guitarists may have similarities in their playing but it does not necessarily outline a style. It is easy to hear the influence Charlie Patton had on his contemporaries in the Mississippi Delta or the impact that Blind Blake had on the guitarists in the Carolinas. And, for example, the specifics of guitar tunings and harmonic ideas are common to the playing of most guitarists from St Louis. But when one listens to the music of Charlie Patton, Mississippi John Hurt, Bo Carter and Robert Johnson – all from the Delta area – it is equally easy to hear how completely different their paying was from each other in terms of approach, sound, lyrics, rhythmic feel, and choice of tunings. The music of Texas musicians such as Blind Lemon Jefferson, Mance Lipscomb,[19] Blind Willie Johnson[20] and Henry Thomas exhibit vastly different approaches. Even in the playing of guitarists whose styles are more closely related, such as Reverend Gary Davis, Blind Boy Fuller[21] and Willie Walker[22] (all from the Carolina area) one can easily discern musical differences, for example the chord voicings they used, the attack, the dynamics, etc. – all the things that help us to identify an individual's style. The nuances of sound and touch as well as the choice of harmonies – in short the essence of the music – are unique to each player.[23]

Even though there sometimes appears to be a dominant song, guitar key, or melodic idea that was adopted in a certain region, categorizing blues music can miss the mark. The main lesson is that the beauty of the music lies in how each individual artist taps into the wellspring of what went before him or her, adds something of him or herself to the mix, and in the process creates something fresh and new. It is a process of assimilation and re-invention – a state of flux and constant renewal. For me, this is the beauty of blues music – and where it originally comes from. It is the sense that each song has a story all of its own but is also an extension of others. The songs refer to each other, grow out of each other – that is the tradition as I see it. Whatever connections the players shared, their recordings demonstrate that even though the initial audience has gone, originality is always at the center of the blues and that is why the music is forever full of possibilities.

My conclusion is that much of what the historians have written is a distraction from what really matters – the music itself and some insight into how these great musicians became masters of their craft.

The other vital question about the early country blues artists that is not addressed directly is " Why did they play?" We can never know for sure what motivated them to play, but I can offer the insights I gleaned first-hand through my lessons with Rev. Gary Davis and when I played with the great blues singer and bottleneck guitar player Son House.

Son House – My Brush With a Blues Legend (or "why play?")

I was 17 years old when I played with Son House.[24] I met him in New York, as part of the Nick Perls scene. Nick was the one who invited Son House to stay at his place. Nick called me up; he wanted to record House. The problem was that Son House really couldn't play well at that time. So Nick wanted me to play guitar and for Son to sing.

So I learned Son's songs, went over to Nick's place and we recorded the session that afternoon. I played and Son sang. He was fighting *delirium tremens,* or the DTs, at the time and was kind of out of it. There wasn't much talking at that session. I don't think he knew where he was – that he was in a studio being recorded. He would hear me play a riff, recognize it and then launch into a tune, then stop suddenly and look really dazed and confused. Then I would start playing the guitar part to one of his songs and he would come back to life.

I would play, he would sing louder, and I would play louder – and we would go back and forth. It was an amazing experience and a strange but strong musical connection. The one thing that stands out in that memory is the power and volume of his voice. It made me play stronger and in new ways just to keep up.

He had no method or approach to the music that I could discern, at least not at that session. It was totally spontaneous. He wouldn't even talk about the tune we were about to play. He didn't seem to have any sense of form; it was very free flowing. Most of the tunes we recorded were truncated, literally "chopped off." For example, we would play for two or three minutes and then it would simply trail off. So we would use those stretches for a final take. On the one hand, it was just like a stream of consciousness, but on the other hand, there has to be a question mark over whether illness, dementia, or other mental health issues were impacting on his ability to communicate and perform. All that I remember is that we knew for sure he was not going to last. But he survived for another fifteen years (Son died in 1988), which given his condition when we made those recordings in 1971 and 1972[25] was astounding; the strength of the man. I mean, he really was one of *the* performers back then. He was *the* singer-player, if not the greatest, then one of the greatest, for sure.

You really did get the feeling that when he was younger he was just, like, "Wow". Even back in 1972 he was physically in bad shape and not really together, the power of his music came across so naturally. All I remember is just flailing at the guitar – and I was playing a metal-bodied guitar made by National that day – just going at it as hard and as fast as I could. I got the feeling that must have been what it was like to perform back then. You know, Son would just get into the mood, and this frenetic thing would happen. Just amazing. Very full out; fifth gear all the way. It is probably the closest throwback to him playing in a barn dance or a country dance hall that I could get to experience. I think that all of those types of players, the Charlie Patton's, Willie Brown's, when they played back then, it was just full on, all out, full stop. They played for a reason. A job. That job could be a dance, a church, a street to play, but always to earn money. There was always a reason to play. At least that's the impression I got. They would play for medicine shows, to be funny or for laughs; they played to entertain – but always for money. Everything about the music had purpose and that gave it a cutting edge. It was not approached as an 'art form' – it was more like "play because you have to". Back then even jazz was not considered art or "good music." Jazz players were considered drug addicts or outcasts at best, so you can imagine how blues players were thought of. Blues is great art – but back then it wasn't great art to the musicians. What was Son's purpose for playing that day? Perhaps it was habit? It was about survival – that much was obvious to me.

The results of that recording session were released on the record "Been Here and Gone" which also contains a number of recordings I made around the same time, also in Nick's kitchen, with the English singer Jo Ann Kelly. It is a record that holds a lot of happy memories for me.

Finding Purpose in Your Playing

As exhilarating as it was to cut a record with Son House, for me it always comes back to Rev. Gary Davis. As important as any riff or idea he showed me on the guitar was how he found a purpose and a drive to his playing. When Davis was playing, he was preaching. He preached with total conviction. This underpinned his music and gave it much of its energy – this was the power behind his music. Every audience was his congregation.

I did go to Davis's church – not often. In truth, I found it a little freaky. The church was located in a condemned movie theatre. I recall the congregation – the women in gloves and pink outfits, the men in their morning suits. There were usually about 30 to 40 people who occupied the first two rows of seats in the auditorium. On the first occasion Sister Annie Davis asked me to play – so I played *Say No To The Devil*, the only tune I could really get through at the time. I was as nervous as hell and started off playing and singing timidly. But I realized as I was stood there that they were only interested in the song. They were not looking at me – in fact most of them had their eyes shut. So that relaxed me, and it became a cool experience. So there was the lesson – it wasn't about me, it wasn't about me standing there with a guitar trying to impress people. They were there for the songs only, as part of their prayer or religious experience.

Looking back, the message was simple. The purpose in music is beyond merely producing a set of notes – there has to be a wider purpose to it than just getting from the start of a tune to its end. Kenny Werner[26], the jazz piano player, puts it another way:

"...you have to discover a reason for living that is more important than playing! You need a sense of self that is stable, durable and not attached to your last solo. And paradoxically that makes you better! It removes the consequences and puts everything into perspective. The pressure is gone... and you play better."

He doesn't necessarily express the idea in the same language that Davis would have used himself, but I think that the example of Davis says the same thing. Davis was a "believer" and his music was performed, ultimately, in the service of his belief in God. His music supported that conviction, and his religious enthusiasm underpinned his music. A very powerful symbiosis – and this lay at the heart of the message he communicated through his music.

Finding Integrity in Music and in Life

I always had a special feeling about Davis – like I was part of his family. His influence on me extended beyond the tunes that I learned at my guitar lessons. At least as impressive as his musicianship was the man himself. This was a man who had known harsh times, but I never heard him complain about his life, or about being poor. He had no bitterness about getting old and not being recognized. Davis was comfortable and content with who he was. He seemed like a man at peace, which is unusual for someone who had such a hard a life. Inspirational really.

The greatest lesson I am still learning from Davis is, ultimately, his example of how to just be who you are and believe in it, of how to live a good life. He led a hard life but managed to maintain his integrity and his dignity throughout the years.

On Reflection...

Davis' music hits me on the same level as the music of Lennie Tristano or Carlos Paredes. It's visceral, direct, un-hung up music, which is created for it's own sake. It is not filtered through conversations. It is not intellectual music. As Lennie used to say: "Don't be afraid to sit on your dick." In other words, just sit down and fucking play – don't think. And what he meant by that is, don't adjust yourself, don't try to filter what you are playing – just play.

And I think Davis was the same – that is the connection.

So I played with Davis and studied with him, right up until he died in May of 1972. And after he died I stopped playing his music – for nearly 15 years. That is not to say I forgot about him. It's that I was hearing something else. I was done, for the time being, with the finger-style blues world. By that stage, I was bored actually. Not of the music (and music scene) but I was looking to study something else – jazz logically – but the problem was that I really didn't like the modern jazz that I heard. At that time I was into the old Johnny Dodds stuff, which came from my interest in the clarinet. In a way, I was in the same place that I was in when I first met Davis; I was looking for a way forward, but didn't have a road map or even a compass to direct me to the next thing. I heard the name 'Lennie Tristano' and without really knowing his music (or liking it), I went out to his house for a lesson. I was just grasping at straws...

Rev. Gary Davis

Son House

With Bukka White

With Jo Ann Kelly

Chapter 2

Into the Maelstrom: Lennie Tristano

"Just remember, never forget you play music because you love it. That's the reason you play. Always stay in touch with that feeling. That's why you play. That's what music is."

If Lennie were alive today I would probably be studying with him.

Finding Lennie – Another Awakening

What is the appropriate way to introduce Lennie? In short, He was one of the greatest improvisational musicians who ever lived. Unusual for such a great performer, Lennie took his teaching equally as seriously. A brief biography does not capture the essence of the man, but for the sake of context Lennie (full name Leonard Joseph Tristano) was born on March 19, 1919, a native of Chicago to parents of Italian origins.[27] Born with extremely poor eyesight, he was completely blind by the age of six years. He studied at the American Conservatory of Music in Chicago, graduating with a BA in music in 1943. During his years in Chicago he started teaching – amongst his earliest students was the great alto-saxophone player Lee Konitz. Lennie relocated to New York in 1946, quickly establishing himself on the burgeoning jazz scene. He was a contemporary of Charlie Parker, Bud Powell and Dizzy Gillespie – part of that generation of jazz innovators – performing regularly with them as well as leading his own group predominately made up of his own students – Lee Konitz, Warne Marsh, Peter Ind and Billy Bauer being among the best known of the first wave, or generation, of Lennie's students. Back in the late 1940s Lennie was at the center of the jazz mainstream. He established a studio on 32nd Street, Manhattan, which became the focus of his recording and teaching activities during the late 1940s and the 1950s. Lennie was forced to move out of this studio in 1956; in classic Manhattan style, the building was demolished and was eventually redeveloped. He moved out to Queens, New York where, as his profile as a performer waned, his teaching became the main focus of his activities. Lennie died from a heart attack on November 18, 1978.

At the time I started going to lessons with Lennie, I was actually looking for a guitar teacher. I went to Chuck Wayne for a few lessons. I went to a few others. I wanted to learn "jazz guitar" and these were the jazz guitar players. It just seemed very intellectual to me. I couldn't get my head around all the modes, scales and how to make music with all that. At that time I was playing early blues and Dixie-land kind of stuff. But I could not get into bebop. I just didn't get it. I could not hear it.

Before I studied with Lennie, I remember asking the jazz musicians I knew about him and almost without exception they said, "Oh he's a genius but be careful, he's also a monster. He'll brainwash you and it's not good." I had no idea what they were talking about and I could not understand how a piano player could teach me guitar. I figured that I had little to lose by going to him and checking it out. None of the other approaches were working for me; jazz and bebop were still a mystery. I was searching.

Lennie lived in Jamaica, Queens, not far from the Reverend's house.

I hadn't been out there since Davis died in '72. I remember driving up to his house and seeing this guy wearing an overcoat waving a baseball bat. It was Lennie. He was trying to catch a neighbor's dog that was chasing and scaring his students. There was Lennie, baseball bat in hand, a blind man leading me in through the back walk path to his upstairs apartment. When we made it to his teaching room he asked me to play for him. I launched into a few Gary Davis tunes and a country blues song. He said "Now I'll really get you into music" – as if the music I played for him was not music. He just totally dismissed it. It completely 'weird-ed' me out and at the time I just thought it was not "hip" enough for him. I found out later what he really meant. I was trying to impress him with my chops and speed and it was not about the tune or style I was playing, it was the *way* I was playing it. For a while I had the sense that there was something missing in my music and here was the person who could show me the way forward. I was unaware at that moment that I was embarking on a whole new journey with one of the greatest improvising musicians who has ever lived. It was an amazing experience. He opened my ears up and totally transformed my whole sensibility of music. He was great teacher.

Lennie definitely interviewed you. I remember going out for that first meeting. I played for him and I talked with him. But he didn't say, "You passed." I don't remember exactly what he said, but it was along the lines of, "If you're going to study with me, here's how it works. You come out here, do what I tell you. This is what I charge. Let's get you into music." I didn't really understand his approach to teaching but something made me want to see what is was all about. I knew he was famous in the jazz world, and I knew of some of his other students who were great players in their own right. I thought "there must be something here and I'm not getting it." Perhaps I was just stubborn. We started the lessons the following week. And so I spent half my youth on that damn subway out there, to the end of the 'E' train subway line at Jamaica, Queens.

I never thought to ask Lennie the question, "Where did you get your approach from?" but I always felt that Lennie got his insights, the basis of his approach to playing and teaching, from his experiences being at the center of the 1940s and early 1950s jazz scene in New York. That was a tough life. It was very immediate because it required musicians to react on the spot to a new tune, a new set of changes to a standard tune, perhaps even a novel harmonic concept often taking place on the bandstand. And his teaching method of playing in the moment and playing the shit out of every note came from being around the likes of Bud Powell and Bird. His teaching was so natural and direct.

Honesty

A lot of his students, myself included, would go into his house and try to impress him. We would try to play fast and he would always say, "Don't try to impress me," often followed by, "I've heard it all before, don't try to bullshit me." I would just be playing something and he would say, "Stop bullshitting," and I'm like, "what are you talking about?" I didn't know what he was talking about and I would say, "What?, I'm playing!" And he would say, "get out of my house." I would usually protest, "I'm not bullshitting, I'm just playing." And he would snap-back straight away, "No, you are bullshitting me." Eventually, I realized he was right: I was trying to impress him.

Lennie's whole thing was to just get to the music. It was all about the music, not about talking about it or all the peripheral stuff. When you are a kid, you don't necessarily understand that. I just didn't know what he was talking about. I thought I knew the words, the notes etc. I thought he was just nuts or crazy or something: "Who is this guy?" or "He's just eccentric," or "What is he talking about?" Many times I would leave a lesson and he would say: "You don't have that, do it again next week." But I thought that I had it perfect:

– *"But Lennie, I know it."*
– *"No you don't, come back next week."*

- *"What do you mean, I'm not..."*
- *"See you next week. Do it again."*

He would not tell me why I wasn't playing it perfectly. I would go home and think, "Why is he doing this? He just wants to get rid of me." I did not understand what it was about. Of course, now I realize that it was about knowing what you were doing and feeling it, and not bullshitting. When you are young you are full of self-consciousness about your image of yourself. You are trying to impress people, trying to impress the teacher, trying to impress women, all of that stuff. And to go to someone who just cuts to the quick like that is real wake-up call. If you can hear it. I think many of Lennie's students left him after only a handful of lessons.

There is Nothing Magic About the Process of Learning

The process with Lennie was very slow. We never discussed theory or concepts. Every time I asked the question, "What will we be working on next, what tune, what chord voicing, what scale?" he wouldn't answer me. "Just do your work", he would say.

Studying with Lennie taught me that getting into jazz is a slow process. You first need to open up your ears, to become receptive to it. There is no mystery – it is just about taking your time and feeling your way into it. It isn't an intellectual process. Looking back, it is almost as if the first year of my studies with Lennie were about the music, but it wasn't about the guitar or even any instrument. It was about getting exposed to new music, and playing in a way that I had never done before. Playing slowly. For example, I went to music school so I knew the theory of scales, seventh chords and all that stuff, but I could not put it onto the guitar. So a lot of the process was about simply slowing down, and also getting away from that conversation you have with yourself at 21 years old, which is like "Hey, I'm cool." Lennie cut through all that: "You're not cool, fuck you, I've seen it all. You can't even play a triad."

That first year was really strange. I don't think I had a lesson that lasted more than twenty minutes. I would travel out to his place on the subway, one and a half hours, with my guitar and then have to walk a mile to his house where I'd sit in his waiting room until called for my lesson. Typically I would sing a solo that I had learned beforehand using headphones, or sitting near the speaker, with one ear covered and the other open so I could hear myself sing. The idea of singing the solos of great musicians (typically with Lennie a solo by the saxophone player Lester Young or the guitarist Charlie Christian) was not just to copy the notes correctly, but also to absorb and internalize the nuances of phrasing, tone, emphasis, accent and feel – in short to learn the whole of the jazz language, and most important to Lennie, the feeling of jazz. Then I would play a melody with the metronome, just one melody, one chorus, no improvising. Then I'd run through a couple of scales, perhaps some interval work. All played very slowly. The idea was that to play fluidly and fast, you first needed to be able to play very slowly and that in time with a metronome. And that was it, "See you next week." No improvising, no playing together, no nothing for a whole year. Many times I would leave his house and I'd sit on his front lawn thinking, "What am I doing?" I would almost be in tears, like, "He doesn't like me, why is that?" But I kept going back. Gradually the lessons started to take over my life and for me it was a great experience, because before I got into the music, I got in into the head. The groundwork.

Part of the reason why I think Lennie was such a good teacher is that he wasn't trying to please you. He wasn't trying to make you stay with him. He wasn't trying to feed your ego. His mindset was just, "This is how you learn. If you don't like it, great, goodbye." Most teachers will not do that. It is about wanting to please your client. Lennie was in a place where he had enough students. He didn't care if you stayed with him or left. I mean, he told me to stop taking lessons many times. He said to me, "I don't need your money, I don't want to teach you anymore." Other times he'd say, "Just get out, no problem, goodbye. If you are not going to do what I say, goodbye. No hard feelings. Ciao. You don't have to study with me." That was it. And I could have left at any time.

It is Not About Copying a Style or a Sound – The Idea is to Get Deeper Into Your Own Sound

I think Lennie's jazz-is-a-feeling-not-a-sound approach to approach to playing was under-appreciated. Partly this is because it was not mainstream. Pure improvisation is very individualistic. Lennie played with Charlie Parker, and his students, Lee Konitz, Warne Marsh, Sal Mosca, as well as with Fats Navarro and Bud Powell. They could all play with the beboppers, but they all played in their way, and that's the beauty of jazz. It's about creative individuality. And to me what Lennie was doing was really keeping the jazz tradition alive. That's why he didn't create a school of musicians who were "off the shelf" – cut from the same jazz cookie cutter. It was the same with Warne Marsh. He could play any standard in the book, so he could play on the bandstand with straight beboppers, but he would play his own way.

Many jazz teachers teach a method. I never learned a "jazz guitar method" with Lennie. It's strange, you know, I'm a jazz guitarist but I never studied Wes Montgomery, Joe Pass, or Jim Hall (although I loved their music). I learned the standards and I learned some solos and lines but not the regular jazz guitar licks and stuff. Sometimes I'll hear something and think, "Oh, that's a cool sound. I'll try to figure out what that is." But, you know, there's a whole approach and methodology to jazz guitar playing and developing standard jazz techniques. I just have Lennie's approach; learn how to hear music, then the shit-work and then how to improvise. There are plenty of methods for guitar: here's your blues method, here's how you substitute chords etc. You don't learn how to listen and bring your ear into alignment with your mind and chops. Your fingers follow the method, and it's more difficult to play what you feel or what hear in your mind. That's why singing is important. Lennie used to say, "If you can't play during the week, sing." He said, "The most important thing is don't lose touch with your playing feeling." That was his big thing. You don't have to have the guitar in your hands but sing, sing your solo. Make a solo tape of all the solos you sing and constantly go over them – internalize them. Again and again. And you wouldn't play it on the guitar, you'd just sing it. Put a speaker in one ear and sing along with the record. So you'd sing live for him. I'd sit in front of the speaker put the tape on and then I'd sing with the speaker going at the same time. "That's the most important thing you can do if you want to stay in touch with your "playing feeling." Singing is the most important thing... and it's fun. If you do that you can't lose. And sing everything at half speed. I would ask, "What do I sing to" and Lennie would reel of a bunch of names: Bird, Bud, Fats, Charlie, Prez. So I started listening. Lester Young, Charlie Christian, Fats Navarro, Bud Powell. Each week I would sing one of their solos. I started with Charlie Christian. His guitar style was bluesy so I could hear it. There is nothing like singing Charlie at half speed.

It is About "Not Thinking"

Lennie's approach to music was not intellectual. Yes, there was a method, for example, the exercises were highly organized and the work was broken down into sections to be worked on. But ultimately Lennie's whole trip was to get to that place where the music is about feeling rather than thinking. He used to say; it's impossible to think and really play music at the same time.

When I look back on that first year of lessons with Lennie, the big mystery for me is what actually happened in that year. And it really was a year, one year almost to the day. I didn't become a better musician or any of that stuff. It's just that everything I listened to clicked. And it wasn't like an intellectual response: "Oh, now I appreciate it." It was instead totally emotional. It was as if all of a sudden the world opened up and hearing this new music was like, "Wow! This is what I've been waiting to hear my whole life." It was as if somebody pulled the cover off and there it was. It was amazing. It wasn't about your training, it wasn't just about listening; it was about becoming receptive to the music on a feeling level. I think after that year of singing and slow study I was just ready for it, "Oh right, of course!" Just "boom" and I could hear the melody through the improvisation: "Oh right, got it. I hear what you are saying…"

**Aligning the Ear, the Mind and Your Chops –
"Bringing it All Together"**

Once your ears are really open, bringing your chops and your brain into alignment is a slow process. Basically, you play so slow that you ended up hearing and 'physicalizing' each note. I don't think there was any kind of magical theory in Lennie's teaching. It was just like, play your triads and hear it. If it takes you six months to master one triad, that's how long it takes you. You know, that's the magic. There were no shortcuts, no new postulate of theory or hip jazz patterns. Just learn the intervals, triads, seventh chords in all keys, play it slow…

Understanding theory doesn't help you play. There is no concept of a 'correct' theoretical way to play. Theory is only a way of explaining what you have already done. So, to learn theory first and to say, "Oh, I need to learn theory to play," is back-to-front thinking. It is like teaching the blues and the pentatonic scale – the "blues scale." The blues scale developed out of players thinking, "lets organize how to play blues with a system; we'll call it the pentatonic blues scale." But it's after the fact, so how can you first learn the pentatonic scale to play blues? It's actually doing it backwards. You can't intellectualize it: "Oh, a fourth interval is seven semi-tones." What does that mean? "A dominant seventh chord is made up of the root-third-fifth-flattened seventh." It doesn't mean anything until you hear it. Without sound, there can't be any theory. The sound and the music – that came first.

There was a real disconnect when I was going to school, taking theory tests and analyzing Mozart scores. One day I would be playing the Spohr and the Weber clarinet concerto, the next day working on a Blind Blake solo. I could not relate my schoolwork with blues and folk music. Studying with Lennie was such a slow process – so much repetition – that I started to hear the theory. Basically, you cannot circumvent the process. You cannot use theory as a substitute for putting in the time so that you learn to hear and feel what you are playing. If you cannot hear it, then you cannot really play it. Period. Jazz is not a secret technical language. The technique and the theory are just there to support the music, never as an end in itself.

Learning the Basics – "Shit-work is the Key to Effortless Mastery"

When I think about it, I really didn't study jazz with Lennie. It was just music. Along with opening up my ears by listening and singing solos I did the guitar keyboard work; intervals, triads, 7th chords, articulation and rhythm exercises – what he called the "shit-work". This started with the first lesson. I did all the keyboard harmony work, the ear training, singing solos etc. When you sing the melodies, sing along to solos, that's when you get ideas. You just soak it in. You hear the melodies, you hear the rhythm, and you hear the nuances. For example, I would take eight bars of a solo and sing those eight bars for four weeks. Just eight bars, taking it slowly. It wasn't about how much you did it or how many times you did it, it was about the quality of it. You do your shit-work, your ear training, you learn your melody, and after a while it just sort of works. It's magic in the way it just comes together. But no one said, "here's your lick." So what comes out is improvisation, you're hearing the melody and playing something else, you are not getting lost in the form; you are improvising. If you learn that approach it's going to come out sounding very different to a jazz formula guitar method book.

I think that Lennie had a certain program, like the shit-work for instance. You do your scales, all the intervals; second, thirds, fourths, fifths etc. You played all of these in all twelve keys, major and minor. I'm talking about major, harmonic minor, melodic minor scales; all the intervals in all twelve keys. Then the triads; close voice – 'one-three-five', 'three-five-one', 'five-one-three'; then do the open voices – 'one-five-three', 'three-five-one' etc.

So, you do six open voices in majors or minors, and to get that perfect, that's a chunk. If you are doing six keys a week, then do the maths. Fifty two weeks in a year. Just break it up – it's like, there's two year's work for you right there. And then you've got the seventh chords; one-three-five-seven closed voice; three-five-seven-one open voices, so there is a set of voicing's on the guitar that you can do. And I'd say to Lennie:

- *"What about this voicing?"*
- *"Don't ask me, just play it."*
- *"Sometimes we can't do this on the guitar"*
- *"Well don't do it - Do the chord. I want to hear three-seven-five-one."*
- *"I can't reach it".*
- *"Well do the best you can. I'm not a guitar player."*

So you do your voicings, diatonic, all twelve keys, for the seventh chords. Then you get to your ninth chords, and then you get to your altered chords. So I think Lennie did have a program. And on piano, I think that was a little different – there was definitely a pedantic kind of curriculum approach to the technical keyboard theory.

When it came to shit-work all I studied were triads, scales, intervals, seventh chords. None of this is rocket science. I would sit in his teaching room and I would play, for example, a series of seventh chords: "OK, see you next week." The next week, it was the same again. Just playing the scales slowly, major scales, melodic minor, harmonic minor, up and down all the keys. Each week I would do the sharp keys, two or three keys. So it was slow, very slow. And I think that was the whole thing. Then after about a year into my lessons he said, "Now improvise." But for that first year I was playing melodies straight, against the metronome, no vibrato, no foot tapping, no string bending, just playing the fucking melody. He kept saying, "Just play the fucking melody." If I wanted to learn anything else, he said, "Just learn it." I said, "What songs should I learn?" He said, "I don't know, just pick a song." It was difficult at the time because I had a lot of friends learning jazz guitar, and they were learning all the Joe Pass stuff and all the hip Wes Montgomery and Miles tunes. I felt very inadequate, particularly at jam sessions because I wasn't learning the repertoire or all the standard II V I progressions and basic jazz riffs, none of that stuff. I would go to Lennie and say, "Lennie, all my friends are playing jazz and doing gigs." He said, "What do you want me to do?" I said "I don't know. I'm studying jazz with you." He says "Well, if you want to go learn that shit, go learn it. But when you're here, you do what I tell you or you get the fuck out of my house." So I learned to just shut up. I never asked him any more questions because he would never answer me. He said, "So if you want that, go learn it; go learn it, but don't bring that shit here; go learn it, get a book, learn it yourself." He had his own approach of learning music and learning to improvise.

How to Practice

With Lennie you learned at your own pace. You did what you did. But if you went in with excuses he'd say, "See you next week. Pay me 50 bucks." That's it. Oh yeah. I'd go in sometimes, "Oh, I didn't play I had a fight with my girlfriend," you know, "something happened in school," you know, "I can't pay my rent..."

He would go:

- *"You talking to me?"*
- *"Yeah, I just explained it."*
- *"Out!"*
- *"Lennie, what's that?"*
- *"Out, I don't want to hear your bullshit. I don't want to hear

your excuses. Either play me your A flat scale, or if you can't play it, get the fuck out of my house."

Just like that, I mean, just like that. And I'd be like, "Lennie, I thought we're friends." It's the same thing. Either you play your scale or you don't. And if you didn't play it, he would throw you out: "I'll see you next week." And looking back he was right. If I played this scale and played it with just one little fluffed note, he would like, "See you next week – you don't know it." I would say, "Lennie, I just made a little mistake." He would retort, "That means you don't know it." His reasoning was impeccable: he said, "If you know it, you can't make a mistake." Lennie used to say, "If you can't play it, you don't know it. You can't possibly make a mistake if you know something." You can't, it's impossible. And Lennie was right. If you know something, it's impossible. That's why if you know a tune, it's impossible to get lost. If you lose the form, then you don't know it. I think there are certain craft things that are important as a discipline. But then there is also the philosophical aspect of it, like, playing slow, getting in touch with your feelings, getting rid of the head trip.

He was strict about what he required you to do before you moved to the next stage. Typically I would go to my lesson and he'd have me write down my work for the next week, because I was all over the place. He said, "I want you to write down what you practice this week, every day." He meant the shit-work, the melody and what solo I was singing. And the shit-work would be like, this week I'd be doing the sharp keys and I'd be doing open inversion triads, sharp keys, and I'd be doing the intervals in the flat keys or two keys, intervals of the fourth. So I'd write it down. So Monday, you know C and G triads. Tuesday, F and B flat, intervals of a fourth. Tuesday... I'd write it down. So I'd go into my next lesson and then he'd have me time it. He'd say, "I want you to sit there with a timer." And he would say, "I want you to tell me how many minutes you played every day." So for a while I'd go in and he'd say, "what did you play?" and I'd say "I played my flat keys this week in sixths. He goes "How much time did you spend on them?" I said "I spent fifteen minutes on Monday, eighteen minutes on Tuesday, thirty minutes on Wednesday", to the minute, not just approximately. He wanted to know how long to the minute, and I sat there with a parking timer.

So I had a parking timer that gave off a little tic, tic, tic. I'd set it and I'd practice. And I'd work 20 minutes, 17 minutes, I mean to the minute. It is really a good discipline and I kept a log for a long time. I still have my logs from my lessons and it was really, really helpful. And once I was in that habit, then one time I came into my lesson as usual, and he said "Oh great, good job, so how much of it felt good?" And I remember saying, "none of it really felt good. He then said, "None of it felt good?" He said, "what about your soul?" I'd go, "Ah, didn't feel so good." Typical student stuff. And then I said, "Well, you know last Tuesday I was playing, you know Cherokee and the last couple of choruses then all of a sudden it just took off and it felt great. And then I caught myself and thought about it. I came back and felt like shit, you know." He just said, "Oh, so for the whole week you played like a couple of choruses and it felt really, really good?" "Yeah." And he said, "Ah, you had a good week." Boom. He said, "What do you think, you are supposed to feel good all the time? That's what he kept saying. He said "The fuck, you expect satisfaction, just fucking play." He said "You know you're going be fucked up if you play, you're going to be fucked up if you don't play, so just play." That was his whole thing. So there is certain logic in that. "Where do we get this expectation of every time we play it is going to feel good. Every time you take a shit it's going to feel good or bad, but you gotta still shit." That's what he kept saying the whole time, "You just fucking play. Don't think." You know, don't think that's the thing. The minute your brain gets involved you're fucked. It's really true and we're our own worst enemy. If you meet anybody, any musician you meet anywhere, that is the first thing they'll say. I frequently hear students complain "Oh, I got the wife and kids now, I can't play." It's the brain kicking in. Instead of just saying instead, "Oh, I had a few spare minutes. I picked up the guitar." Like nobody has ten minutes in their lives they can play guitar? But they don't do it because the brain interferes: "Oh, what's ten minutes. I'm never going to get good." So you don't do it. Even there the thinking fucks you up. You know, you could have five kids, four jobs, five mortgages, and you can't have ten minutes to pick up the guitar in a week? But they don't do it because, "Why should I do that. I'm just going to be frustrated. I'm not going to be any good so I'll just give it up." On every level the brain gets in the way, instead of just saying, "Hey, this is fun. I'm going to check it out, you know. I've got ten minutes so I'll play some music – cool, I'm having fun." And that is what this 'Effortless Mastery' is about; getting rid of the conversation when you practice the guitar. Some of the things you might say are; "Uh I'm so rough and my hands are stiff, I should've learned that, what's that melody? I should've learned that tune, oh man, I should've done this ten years ago. Who am I? Oh shit, the guitar needs a new string." I mean you can go on and on. That's the thing, getting rid of all that. Just picking it up and saying "I'm great, every note is beautiful." No judgment: you enjoy the joy of it.

All we can do is to be focused on whatever passion moves us and stay in it. One note at a time, keeping the demons at bay. Like a dark quicksand they may be the reason we pursue, but as we sludge through the daily work we now and then discover that we have something to say. It's those fleeting moments of quiet joy that keeps us going... re-affirming who we are... one note at a time.

Playing From the Id, Not the Ego

Lennie later said to me, "You know that first year I really couldn't talk with you because it was all bullshit." And after that he started opening up and talking more, and we had more of a relationship. It's a simple lesson but it's hard. It's about getting rid of that conversation with yourself – the white noise: "Oh, I haven't played for a week, I didn't have the time, my job got in the way, etc." It is about just saying, "Don't judge yourself and don't put stones in your path." If you play consistently, it helps to minimize the conversation. I've known that for years; it's an old friend. If I don't play for two or three weeks, I pick up the guitar and the conversation is an hour. And then if I play, it takes me about an hour to get to the place where, "Ah, this is fun." And then if I play every day, it gets shorter, down to ten minutes of conversation. I even let myself do it. OK, the first ten minutes, negative, negative, negative and getting it out of my system, negative, negative, very good. Then after a while, I just start playing – I'm not even necessarily aware of what I am playing. The conversation just stops and then music can happen, "All right, I'm cool, cool, great." Then I can get into the music. So I have this whole process of getting away from that conversation. So, I've known it, it's such a friend now that I know it and I allow it. So I don't let the negativity try to get to me, but it's not easy. Even at a concert, to not try to impress, just to play and be in the moment. You know, Lennie would say, "Well, before you start a tune, don't just go one, two, three, four... How do you feel? What's the tempo? Just give yourself a second. Where do you feel the tempo?" We don't do that, you know. It's like you don't just jump in the ocean, you walk in, you know, you take your time; feel the tempo. That's why a lot of Lennie's music, he kind of feels his way in, like Warne Marsh, and all of a sudden he latches on. So the first two choruses are just whatever, and then *whoosh* and you pick it up. So it's a process. I think that's where Lennie was coming from, without actually putting it into these terms.

He used to have this thing about playing from the id and the ego, which is a little different idea, but it is the same concept of not letting your ego get in the way. He would talk about the ego and the id, how you should just play the notes from your feelings not your emotions. I think Lennie had an intuitive instinct for how people actually think. I think that's quite a gift. But above all, I think he was just into music. Playing music is a very strange thing because it's really hard to not let your ego get caught up in it. It's really hard, and not just caught up in terms of, "Am I any good?" but also, "Am I getting recognition I deserve?" There's all sorts of levels of ego whether it's societal ego, personal ego or there's this "where's your place?" So, that's why a lot of these great guys isolated themselves.

I was with Lennie for four years and it felt like I was just paying my dues, laying down the basics. By that time I was beyond just getting started. I had made a lot of progress in those four years, but it felt at that time that our work and my relationship with Lennie was shifting somehow. I don't know where it would have gone – it would have been interesting to see – I just ran out of time with him. At around this time, Lennie started having recitals at his house, and that was the "Lennie scene." He hosted house concerts on Sunday afternoons. That was where I first heard some of his other students, who were brilliant. Musicians like Kazzrie Jaxon and Connie Crothers. I have never heard such great music as I did when I was in his house. It was amazing stuff. I heard about it first and he didn't invite me. So when finally he invited me, I felt like, "I'm in." The first thing he said to me, he says, "No shooting up in the bathroom and keep your hands off the women." I said, "Lennie, it's me, the little Jewish kid from Long Island." He said, "No shooting up in the bathroom." And he was serious. I said, "Lennie, what are you talking about?" He said "Oh fuck you, no shooting up." That's so funny. It shows you the world he came from; it was very... it was different.

At that time he kept asking, "How old are you?" He kept asking, "How old are you?" I said, "Twenty." He said, "You're a kid, you're OK." Finally I asked, "Lennie why do you keep asking me how old I am?" His response was typically direct: "Well, I've been teaching my whole life and if I get them when they're young they're OK. But, you know, when they start hitting like, you know, their thirties, they start getting married, having kids and all this stuff." He continued: "I don't know, Ego gets in the way. Ego. I don't know, they don't do what I tell them to do, I just don't know what it is, it just doesn't work." He just kept telling me that over and over again. He reasoned that this is because older/adult learners filtered what he was saying; it's like, instead of just doing the task set for them, they go "Why should I do this?" or, "Let me think about this." When you're young it's like, you either do it or get the fuck out my house. When you are older you try to figure out what he is talking about, the questioning: "Exactly, what does it mean? Why should I practice this? Is this any good? Will it progress me?" That's why he just kept saying, "I don't know, I just see it all the time."

The Teacher – A Personal Evaluation of Lennie's Legacy

I think many jazz historians don't know what to do with Lennie. He wasn't black; he wasn't always part of a group of musicians. He didn't fit into a category. So the best that the historians could come up with was to identify him as part of a "cool school." And it is a similar thing with Warne Marsh. Basically this represents a failure of imagination on their part.

Lennie was central to the jazz world at one time; I am thinking of the ten year period from 1945 through to 1955. Lennie came up playing. Just listen to his early recordings where he played straight ahead. Those live radio broadcast recordings with Charlie Parker – you must hear them. Other recordings I would urge you to check out include the Metronome All Stars recordings with Bud Powell, Lennie, and Max Roach. You hear everybody's solo and then you hear Lennie's solo, and you go, "Whoa, that's so out!" But he's playing a standard tune like *Back Home in Indiana'* and then he has a solo on it. So you could tell even then that he had his own concept of playing. I think that musically he really moved the craft along. I think some people took his ideas, and these ideas are now part of the jazz library, the world over. It was not to the extent of, or at least as visibly as, someone like Bud Powell or Bill Evans. He's not thought of in that way, and I think, again, it gets back to what he was as a performer as a craftsman, as a jazz musician, but also as a teacher. He was just unique; his whole thing with jazz is being original. So whether he is an innovator who could be said to have established a school of jazz, I don't think so. The critics always make reference to the 'cool school', the Lennie Tristano Cool School but I don't really recognize any discernible school. At least, I don't know if people are following the 'school' like they do with, say, bebop. A lot of Lennie's ideas have filtered into education, curriculum and teaching methods. They are there, but they're not acknowledged. You do not sign up to a course on learning Tristano, or even see any acknowledgment elsewhere that this is where it came from. I don't know whether the important question is even whether that's a good thing or a bad thing. In a way, it must be a great thing because it means that at least some of his ideas have been absorbed to the point where you might ask, "how else could you possibly teach it?" So that's quite a powerful thing.

One reason why people don't really teach like Lennie anymore is that I think it is "old school." The way that Lennie taught, you couldn't teach that at a university for instance. It's not fast enough. Imagine for a minute if Lennie was teaching in a college setting – I can almost hear him saying to a student at his or her first day of school, "Learn this melody, learn this scale – see you next semester." His methods don't easily fit into a curriculum designed for a short semester. It's a different thing.

The lesson is the simplicity of it. It's similar to the ideas contained in Kenny Werner's book, *Effortless Mastery*.[26] At the core of it, you can learn the scales and all this stuff but, it's about being in the moment and playing what you hear. How do you teach that? How do you teach someone to be spontaneous, to play what they hear, to play slow? How many teachers today will say to a student "Stop, you're bullshitting yourself." Now, how many people are going to stay there? Like how many of my students would take it from me? I'd go, "No, that's bullshit." They'd go, "Fuck you, I'm playing well." Lennie's approach wouldn't be palatable to everybody. I suppose the flip-side to the argument is that if someone is bullshitting themselves and they don't know they're bull shitting themselves, are they bullshitting themselves? You get these people with these huge egos and they're playing, and we may sit here and go, "Ha, it's all ego." But to them it's not, and who's right? Asking students to submit themselves to a teacher like Lennie, these days it's a hard sell.

It has to be acknowledged that there is also this narrative with some of Lennie's students. Because Lennie was so into music and not trying to school musicians for job placement, I think that a lot of his students got a reputation that they were just, sort of outside the mainstream. There is always going to be that idolatry around someone creative like Lennie. Lennie had this scene around him, because he was such a strong character as a man and as a teacher. He was a powerful figure, so he had students around, there were women around, and inevitably he attracted a kind of scene.

None of that should detract from the core ideas of Lennie's teaching. These are profound and are as legitimate today as they were in the 1940s and 1950s when he first started to develop and expound his ideas.

Further Thoughts on Parallels Between Lennie and Davis

To compare Lennie with other teachers I have had, for example, the few lessons I took with Warne Marsh and Connie Crothers isn't really fair. The closest or most meaningful comparison I could make would be with Gary Davis. But I was much younger when I went to Gary Davis. I really was just a kid then, so my lessons with him had a different dynamic. But it is interesting, Lennie and Davis both lived in Jamaica, Queens, both were blind, living about a mile from each other, and never knew each other. Both were great in their fields but they never met – they occupied totally different worlds. Would they have even understood each other if they had met? I don't know. I think Lennie would have dug Davis because Lennie was just into feeling. It would have been interesting to hear what Davis thought of Lennie too. I wonder if Davis would have understood it or even heard it?

Despite the fact that their roots were evident in their styles, both Lennie and the Reverend were completely original in that they were singular artists whose styles stood out against their contemporaries.

My thinking is that their music was too outside the "normal" musical technical and vocabulary "box" – basically it was too damn hard to play! The influence of both masters is felt by the students they taught, many of whom became more "famous" than they ever were. However, unlike musicians such as Miles, Trane, and Bill Evans, it is far harder to hear the influence of their musical styles in todays jazz and blues music. Other musicians really admired Davis. Lennie's contemporaries acknowledged his prowess as an improvising musician. But stylistically, no one really plays like Lennie today, or even plays his compositions. There are a few exceptions, such as Connie Crothers, Kazzrie Jaxen, and Lennie Popkin who work closely with Lennie's concept, but none of these musicians is widely known today. Lennie knew the jazz language, but he also introduced his own vocabulary to it – just listen to his later recording *The New Tristano* – a unique recording. I cannot think of anything similar to it that has been recorded subsequently. Davis' story has striking parallels – like Lennie he didn't have a broad influence – whatever influence he had is largely the result of his teaching a younger generation of folk musicians during the 1960s. But even then few guitar players really play like Davis.

Warne Marsh – "An Unsung Cat"

Warne Marsh[28]: you hear something great and it lasts you a lifetime. I studied with him briefly after Lennie died. Warne came across as a pretty spacey guy, but he was the most brilliant musician. The guy was unbelievable. I never experienced anyone play music like Warne Marsh.

Warne was one of Lennie's first students during the late 1940s and 1950s. He was a contemporary of Lee Konitz, Sal Mosca and Peter Ind, who were also among Lennie's first wave of students. He was born in Los Angeles on October 26, 1927 into a relatively affluent family. His father was the great Hollywood cinematographer Oliver T. Marsh, who shot stars such as Joan Crawford and Clark Gable. His mother was a violinist.

Personally I think of Warne as being in the same league as Lennie in terms of his level of musicianship and where he took the craft of improvisation. As to why he didn't have a higher profile career, I didn't know him well enough to know what his deal was. All that I know is that it didn't quite happen for him when it came to commercial success or even recognition of his musicianship and insane skills as an improviser. He recorded fairly prolifically during the 1950s, but in my view he suffered when the demand for jazz all but died out in the early 1960s. By the early 1960s the opportunities for a jazz musician were much more limited than in the previous decade, save for a handful of mainstream jazz artists such as Herbie Hancock, Miles Davis, and the like. During the 1960s Warne was living in California and cleaning swimming pools for a living. He died on December 18, 1987 never having received full recognition of his abilities as a phenomenal improvising musician.

On first listening, Warne's music isn't as accessible as the more mainstream jazz performers like Stan Getz, Zoot Sims, or Art Pepper to name a few. He was so far ahead of anybody I've ever heard. I remember some time later when Warne returned to New York to play some concerts. On those occasions his playing was as powerful as Charlie Parker.

In the period after Lennie died, I was searching for a safe mooring, a source of stability to re-ground me at a time in my life when I felt lost, so took a few lessons from Warne. But I didn't learn much from him. He was a very different teacher than Lennie. That is not to say he was a bad teacher – his approach was just different. Warne was very spontaneous. He did not organize his material from lesson to lesson. Mainly his lessons would consist of him sitting with his saxophone demonstrating stuff. He would usually be high, smoking and stuff: "Yeah man, you can take *Cherokee* and, you know, you can play it in B flat, and you can play the upper tones of the chords; and I'll start from the elevenths and go up from there." And I couldn't keep up. He would be playing this unbelievable, unique stuff that I had never heard before. He played not one cliché from a book. His soloing was totally unique and improvised, beautifully swinging and deep. He just didn't play shortcuts or concepts. The whole approach was intuitive.

I remember that he frequently used this expression:

"It's like goin' in to the ocean. You just sort of feel your way and you get your feet wet. You ease in and then you jump in and gotta play and just feel it..."

When you hear his records the first few choruses are easy short phrases but keep on listening and by the third or fourth chorus, he picks up the wave and rides. He's in the form, but he's just making sounds, easy and playing very short phrases. But you just carry on listening, and then at the third or fourth chorus, he just picks up the wave and rides it. He just catches it and he takes off – whoosh – astounding! It is not easy to get hold of his records. Peter Ind has released a few of them on his record label, Wave Records, appropriately enough. He put out Warne's record *'The Art of Improvisation'* – that to my mind is still the bible as far as straight ahead improvisation is concerned.

Warne knew and taught the same themes as Lennie. With Lennie the approach was, "This is what you are doing and if you don't do that, get out of my house." And so you did it. With Warne, he would demonstrate something and say, "Yeah, you can do that if you want to." He didn't demand that you practice anything. Warne just wasn't as pedantic as Lennie was when it came to what you studied with him, at what pace you studied and in what order you covered the material.

In truth, I was intimidated by him – by his sheer musicianship. While it was very cool to hang with Warne, I felt like I was in jazz kindergarten, and I didn't last long as his student. He didn't break down his playing into concepts that I could understand and then later digest and internalize until they became spontaneous. He would demonstrate something and it usually just went over my head. At that time I just didn't have the confidence, skill-set or wherewithal to play with him. He never accompanied me at lessons. We never jammed – I would play whatever exercise he told me to play. And when the time came to start improvising at my lessons, Lennie would just say, "It is your music, play what you want." So when I had to play with Warne during a lesson, I was unprepared. I wasn't used to playing with musicians who were operating at the top level. I was able by then to play a tune, keep time and play a solo, but I was not a seasoned musician. Perhaps this is why I felt as if I was hung out to dry when Lennie died. I'm sure it was part of the reason why I couldn't adapt to Warne's teaching style. I simply wasn't ready for it as a musician. I think I had the same problem when I tried to study with Connie Crothers[29] after I stopped taking lessons with Warne. Connie is a gifted piano player and one of Lennie's protégés. She understood Lennie's teaching approach and musical language. I loved her musical expression but found it a challenge to play with her. I couldn't "hear" her harmonic language. She would play these thick deep polychords that at that time were completely unfamiliar to me and did not resonate. My ears were not there.

Looking back, I wonder whether I was probably too much into Lennie's stuff – too dependent on it in some way. Surely when your teacher dies, it shouldn't devastate you to the extent that Lennie's death affected me. So ever since then I have being trying to find a way back. In retrospect I realize that this placed a near impossible standard for my later teachers, Warne and Connie included, to live up to. Reflecting on these events several years later, my conclusion is that I was just lucky to have the time with Lennie that I had. I am comfortable with leaving it at that. And with Warne too, it doesn't matter so much that my lessons with him didn't develop into a substitute for my lessons with Lennie. I learned many lessons on how to approach improvising just by being around him. Instead I just think of what a great improviser he was.

Chapter 3

Acquiring a Masterpiece

In a book written primarily to acknowledge and pay tribute to great musicians, it might seem slightly odd to give space to guitar builders. Not just any guitar makers, Jimmy D'Aquisto and John Monteleone are perhaps the greatest guitar luthiers of their generation. Both took the craft to a new level, developing what they had learned from the great luthiers before them. The craft of making the instruments, at the highest level, is not unlike the craft of playing music. Like a musician's journey, Jimmy and John made their instruments purely in the service of sound – to get the best sound, tone, texture and nuance out of the box. Their story, like Davis and Lennie is the story of achieving mastery. The dialogue between builder and player is critical. Guitars develop by meeting the demands of the musicians – a fruitful symbiosis, if that dialogue is a constructive and honest dialogue.

Jimmy D'Aquisto

Jimmy D'Aquisto was born in 1935 to a family of Italian origin. At the age of 17, he became an apprentice to the legendary guitar maker

John D'Angelico, who was the premier maker of guitars – the best in the business up until his death in 1964. Jimmy started with the mundane workshop tasks such as sweeping the floor and running errands, and gradually taking on more of the skilled tasks in the process of building a guitar, until he was able to carve the top and back plates, shape the guitar necks and carry out the final instrument set ups. After D'Angelico died, Jimmy set up his own workshop and started to build instruments under his own name.

The Mindset of an Innovator –
My Thinking on Jimmy's Approach to His Craft

If there is one thing you need to remember about Jimmy as a guitar maker, it is that most of his innovations, his ideas about what a top end guitar should be and sound like, are now standard. He took what was there, the tradition that he learned from John D'Angelico, and he moved it forward. Not for the sake of it, but purely in the service of the sound of the instrument. His attitude was "why be bound by tradition if there is a better way to do it?" This ethos was a natural extension of Jimmy's personality – direct, gritty even, but always cutting through grandiose waffle about what a guitar should be or what tradition it belongs to, to what really mattered – the essence of guitar making: sound. He seemed to have little interest in worrying about whether his guitars conformed to a "school" of guitar making. Jimmy would often say, "There is no luthier here, just a guitar maker." For Jimmy it was a never-ending quest to find better ways of building an instrument. Each new instrument was a further refinement of his ideas.

A New Guitar...
At one time I owned a John D'Angelico guitar. A D'Angelico was one of the best acoustic archtop guitars you could get. It was a non-cutaway model – his 'Excel' model — with a dark sunburst finish and more strips of binding (there were six I think) than I've ever seen

on a guitar. As good as it was it needed some work doing to it – the action was too high. I had heard of Jimmy D'Aquisto and got hold of his telephone number, called him up and arranged to go to his workshop on Long Island. I turned up at his place with my D'Angelico – he opened up the case and immediately exclaimed, "I remember that guitar!" He instantly recognized a guitar that he can't have seen for years, and perhaps being one of John's guitars didn't even work on it that much.

Jimmy was a very affable guy. He put a record on and just started to talk about his instruments. At that time some of his terminology was unfamiliar to me. But in a very general sense, he was articulating a lot of things which I had been thinking about: what the sound of a guitar should be, what is a good tone and how is it achieved, and why some guitars are warmer sounding than others, etc.

By the end of that day I remember saying to him, "Jimmy, you are going to have to build me a guitar." The outcome was that I decided not to fix my D'Angelico, but to start on a new guitar instead. I eventually sold the D'Angelico and just went for it. Although this sounds like a straight-forward decision, remember that back in the early 1980's Jimmy had a good reputation as a builder amongst musicians, but his instruments were not then collectible like they are today. To spend $4,000 on one of Jimmy's guitars, especially when I had not even played one of his guitars before that day, was a big deal. You could get a Martin D18 for $500, and at that time Martin was the best flat-top guitar you could get – there were not as many guitar builders as there are today. For me it was hardly possible to buy a $2,000 guitar, let alone a $4,000 instrument. So it was a big deal.

I didn't give any detailed instructions to Jimmy as to what the instrument should be. All we agreed at the outset was that it would be a plain, 17 inch Excel model. There would be no cosmetic adornments – all that mattered was the sound.

In hindsight, given the expense, it looks completely irrational, reckless even to spend that kind of money. But it felt right. This would be a good journey to go on. Within the space of one day, this guy had persuaded me (without him knowing it) to sell my John D'Angelico guitar – then, as now, thought of as one of the best instruments you could get – and to buy a new guitar from a builder whose guitars I had never played. And pay $4k for it! It was nuts, but I was intrigued by Jimmy and his approach to his guitars. And so that day was the beginning of my friendship with Jimmy, and with the start of a whole new learning process.

Talking Wood...

I learned that there are so many variables that potentially have an impact on how a guitar sounds. And the thing you notice after a while is that every instrument maker has his or her pet theories about this, that or the other: when you put all these theories together, they don't really add up. Much of it just doesn't make sense. At least much of it didn't make sense to me, even on an intuitive, non-technical level. They just baffled me. But with Jimmy, his thoughts on how his instruments worked and how they should sound made sense.

One of his theories was "the garden hose theory" which is Jimmy's metaphor for describing how he wanted the sound to project from his guitars. He used to compare the sound coming out of the sound holes to water coming out of a hose pipe. If you do nothing to the hose, the water just dribbles out. But if you squeeze the end of the hose, the water is forced out further – it projects much further. So, for example, he played around with the size and configuration of the sound holes – the f-holes on an acoustic archtop guitar – the idea being to achieve not only volume, but also a good tone – the fatness or warmth of the sound.

Jimmy's 'philosophy' was to pull the most sound out of whatever pieces of wood were put in front of him. When asked what his "criteria" was when building guitars, his response was typically direct:

"Oh, I guess to get the fullest response possible from the instrument. The customer tells me what he wants, but then I forget that. Then I think of what is best for that instrument. How can I get THIS instrument to vibrate and play at its fullest. That's all I think about. THAT instrument. Period."[29]

That ethos drove all of his endeavors when it came to building his instruments. It was about the practice and constant refinement of his ideas in the service of getting the absolute maximum performance out of each of his guitars. Simple.

Jimmy was extremely kind to me over the years, in the first instance as he was building my guitar, and then later on after it was finished. At every stage he took pains to explain everything to me, how the instrument worked, how different parts of the instrument interacted with each other, and why the choice of materials used in the construction of the instrument mattered a great deal, etc. Every aspect of the process was thought out and explained to me. I went out to his house often while he was building my guitar. I did not want to stay long because I knew he was busy, but a short trip would invariably turn into hours of listening to Jimmy's stories. Sometimes I would go out with Nik Munson, my good friend, brother, and great singer. We would just have a laugh-fest hanging out in his workshop, all the while Jimmy demonstrating what he was doing. It was fun. I learned a lot.

Once the guitar was commissioned, the only occasion Jimmy asked for specific input from me was when he reached the point of carving and shaping the neck of the instrument. He just called me up when he was ready and I went out once more to his workshop on Long Island. I tried the neck as it was roughly carved, and on the basis of my feedback, right there in the moment, he just shaved it to its finished thickness and profile in front of me. There was no talk about measurements or specifications – unlike today where the process of even just choosing a factory-made guitar from the shelf of a music store has become far more forensic.

After I had owned the guitar for six months, I took it back to Jimmy's workshop just for him to check it over. I assumed it would be a routine health check. Jimmy picked it up, played it and looked perplexed: "Something is not right. It should be opening up more. I've got to take it back and re-carve the back plate." I couldn't believe it. I said, "Jimmy, the guitar is great. I'm happy with it." But he wouldn't let me take it away. He was adamant that the guitar's sound should have opened up and become warmer, with a more developed bass response. So I returned two months later – and the guitar looked exactly the same. I couldn't see what he had done to it. But once I played it, the guitar was noticeably different. The back was now thinner – so thin I can push the back in and can feel the back of the instrument vibrate when I play it. You really feel it. It is like playing a set of bellows – the top and the back of the instrument pushing against each other to force the sound out.

So while Jimmy had his standard models – the New Yorker and the Excel, and later on the Solo, the Centura, the Avant Garde – each guitar was truly handmade. With Jimmy, it was truly about the customer and the instrument in front of him being made for that customer. It was a very personal process. The end result was completely bespoke – each one of Jimmy's guitars is unique.

Jimmy's obsession with the qualities of sound and tone of his instruments inspired him to achieve a number of groundbreaking advances in the craft of guitar building. His legacy, his gift to music, is these innovations, many of which have become standard in the world of guitar making. You only need to visit a high-end music store to see how many of Jimmy's innovations have been incorporated into the instruments of other guitar builders. It's not always acknowledged openly, but Jimmy's influence is obvious.

John Monteleone – Guitar Heroes

Where was Jimmy taking the archtop guitar? I'm not entirely sure where he would have taken it since I didn't play his last guitars. During the last two years of his life, I didn't see much of him, although we talked over the telephone regularly. I knew he was experimenting, as evidenced by the emergence of a new range of models in addition to the New Yorker and Excel models he used to build. He would talk about the shape of the sound holes, and how he was making them bigger and placing them in different positions, all sorts of innovations were in the pipe-line. The exhibition put on at New York's Metropolitan Museum of Art in 2011, titled "Guitar Heroes" – featuring the artistry of John D'Angelico, Jimmy D'Aquisto, and John Monteleone – gave us a glimpse of Jimmy's later work and one can only speculate as to what future innovations he would have introduced had he not died so suddenly at the age of 59, the same age as his mentor John D'Angelico, when he died.

It was great to see Jimmy's work displayed in the Met Museum. It is strange though to know that when Jimmy was alive he was only known in the guitar world, and that only posthumously is a wider audience now discovering his mastery. Jimmy did not die a wealthy man.

There is a positive ending however. John Monteleone, a builder also working on Long Island, has picked up the conversation where Jimmy left off. John even completed Jimmy's last guitar following Jimmy's death. He understood Jimmy's approach to building guitars but has his own concept of what a guitar should be. John's guitars are built in the service of sound, like Jimmy's guitars, but he also bends the limits of the aesthetics of his instruments, taking the visual/sound connection to a new place. He brings together the sound of the instrument with fine art – an incredibly original artistic vision – not just in terms of his woodwork, but also in terms of the aesthetics of what a guitar should or can look like as a unique work of art. The quality of the sound is still paramount and each new instrument is an innovation in the possibilities of what a guitar can do.

The language which John uses to talk about his instruments is very different to a conversation with Jimmy, but John will sit down, just like Jimmy did, and explain how the instruments work and what he is trying to achieve with the instrument. He knows enough to know that sometimes you can't explain why an instrument sounds a certain way. John is always striving to push the envelope, for example, trying different configurations of sound holes, including innovations such as sound holes placed in the sides of the instrument. The side-ports will probably become a standard feature on instruments in the future – to me they are a no-brainer. Anything that improves the ability of the musician to hear what he or she is playing has to be a good thing.

The exhibition at the Met spotlighted John's skills as a luthier in a way that is, I think, unprecedented – at least for an instrument maker who is still alive. Hopefully this exhibition represented a positive step towards recognizing the abilities of these great craftsmen, respecting their talents and acknowledging the contribution that each of them has made to the music. John's guitars are elegant and have an artistic integrity to them. The flat-top instrument John made for me has a rare elegance to it. This instrument is at another level from all the other flat-tops I have played – it expresses a different concept of what a guitar is than the traditional American Martin or Gibson flat top guitar. It is as if it is in another sonic pocket – as if John has managed to create a new species of the guitar, not just in terms of the sound and tone of the instrument, but also in the way it feels to play. It is closer to a fine Steinway piano in the way it responds to being played and its dynamic spectrum across its entire range – the instrument – each note – feels almost weighted like a piano key. On several occasion I have asked John how he achieved this sound. In his typically modest way he said simply, "I don't know, it is just the way I make them." All I can say is that I have played for a long time and played many guitars, some great, some shitty, all kinds of designs, traditions, experiments, different woods – all looking for something, trying to re-invent the wheel. And then there is John's flat-top guitar, each note like an arrow, solid but like a delicately balanced see-saw, the sound never falls off. At any volume or any attack the note sits bell-like, clear, with a depth and solidity that just makes you want to play and see what comes out next: the surprise of making music. What else can it be but mastery? It is not about re-inventing the wheel. It is about finding the essence. There are guitars and then there is a Monteleone.

When I think of Jimmy, I remember his passion, his musicality and his emotional depth. When I visit John's house I am struck by the elegance and serenity of his workshop, his sheer talent as a craftsman and a creative artist, and I admire how articulate he is. They are very different people, and their instruments reflect that, but to me they are part of the same master craftsman/artist/innovator conversation – they understood and respected each other's talent hugely. Their mastery was individual – ultimately an expression of who they are as people, their values, and their personalities.

*"...No two pieces of wood are the same.
That's the way you have to approach it..."* – *John M.*

John Monteleone

Chapter 4

Other Orbits: The Zoller System

When I was growing up, many children dreamed of becoming astronauts. I didn't share that dream. The closest I ever got to a trip to the outer realms was the time that I spent with Attila Zoller – his world as he called it, "The Zoller System."

For me the essence of that trip was the story of Attila's mastery of his craft through his total focus and dedication to music. It is about the freedom he found within his music. Although Attila's music is very different to Lennie's, both are masters when it comes to rooting out the emotion and meaning inherent in the music they play. And even though he is not particularly well known, his brilliant compositions and his experiments with 'free' (or avant-garde) music are groundbreaking.

Even when he was succumbing to cancer at the end of his life, Attila still mustered the strength to communicate his message in a final recording - his first and only solo guitar record. The title of that CD, "Lasting Love," captures perfectly Attila's feeling towards music – the pure joy he found in it. It is a fitting title. The eleven original compositions set down on this record are a testament to his gift for melody, harmony, improvising and above all, his capacity for communicating feeling through his playing. They represent the final statement of a master musician.

First Reflections

Looking back, it was a shame that I didn't take lessons with Attila. I should have but I didn't. When I met him I was already a professional musician. When I was with Davis and Lennie, I still viewed myself as a student – that kept my ego in check. By the time I was with Attila – in my early to mid-twenties – I was a fledging pro. Perhaps I thought I knew more than I did. I should have studied with Attila. Actually, I tried on many occasions to take a lesson from him but we would end up arguing about something or he would get frustrated with me. Perhaps he thought I knew more than I actually knew at that time.

Attila had a multi-faceted and frequently paradoxical personality, truly an enigma. He had little or no sense of self-censorship. He was like a big kid, but on a good night you could have a ball together. I remember on one occasion driving to his house in Vermont. It was dark and I was trying to follow his car as best I could, but he just disappeared out of sight. I could not keep up with his driving. I then saw his car pulled up in the roadside, so I stopped behind him thinking he had a problem. Attila got out of his car and came steaming down the roadside, the oncoming traffic screaming past him. I wound down my window and he just yelled at me, "Why are you driving so slow…what is wrong with you? I cannot drive that fucking slow". He then got back in his car and stormed off into the distance. He had pulled over on a busy road, late at night, just to yell at me for driving too slowly. So, I carried on driving to his place, at my own pace, but completely on edge as to what state Attila would be in when I arrived. By the time I rolled up at his front door he had completely forgotten about the incident – as if it had never occurred. That was typical of Attila. He was really nuts. But at his core, Attila was a true musician.

He was the guy who got the award from Downbeat magazine, "Talent Deserving Wider Recognition" – twice in two decades.[30] Put simply, he was a brilliant, brilliant musician.

Even in jazz circles, Attila is a relatively obscure figure. He was born in 1927 in Visegrad, Hungary. His father was a professional violinist and he started out playing the violin as child, switching to the flugal-horn, and later to the guitar, during his teenage years. His formal education was disrupted by the Soviet occupation of Hungary at the end of World War II. He escaped Hungary in 1948 just before the Soviets re-occupied Hungary, traveling first to Vienna before moving to Germany in 1954. It was in Germany that he forged important musical associations, many of which would last for the remainder of his lifetime. These included the German pianist Jutta Hipp (to whom he was once engaged), the saxophonist Hans Koller and visiting American musicians such as Oscar Pettiford and the alto saxophonist Lee Konitz. Atilla relocated to the US in 1959 where he undertook formal training at the Lennox School of Jazz. It was there that he encountered Ornette Coleman and Don Cherry, and further developed his interest in 'free jazz.' He played with many of the jazz greats, including Stan Getz, Ron Carter, Red Norvo and Herbie Hancock. Attila died in 1998 after a battle with cancer.

There are two huge lessons I learned from Attila. The first was Attila's ability to retain a childlike enthusiasm for what he was doing – like Lennie, he managed to retain that sense of pure "joy" in his music. Right until the end of his life Attila was excited about music and his playing, for example, the way he could find a childlike joy in finding a new chord. I admired him for that. The second is a more cautionary lesson – the danger of letting your ego cloud your judgment and interfere with what you are doing. This is almost an extension of the conversations I had with Lennie about the id and the ego – except the example of Attila instead shows the traps and pitfalls in real-time, not just as an interesting debate. We all have an ego but the trick is keeping it in check. Sometimes he just couldn't keep it together. I'd see him get into fights with people if he felt he was being slighted. He'd get angry and really pissed off and storm out of a place, storm off the bandstand, not finish a gig. On one occasion he was going to be on a record with the other great jazz guitarists; Jim Hall, Barney Kessell, and Joe Pass, to name a few. On finding out that he was only getting one tune on the record, when the others were getting two tunes each, he flipped out and refused to do the record. Had he done that record, Attila would probably have found a wider audience. He was not a good businessman.

First Contact with Attila

I first met Attila via Jimmy D'Aquisto – when I was trying to sell my D'Angelico guitar. Attila visited me at my apartment on Riverside Drive to try out the guitar. He stayed for a few hours and I was blown away with his playing. We played a few tunes. At that time, I was just getting into my lessons with Lennie, whose approach to improvising was different from the place where Attila was coming from. Attila had a very detail-orientated approach to the guitar –how every chord would be voiced, how it voiced to the next chord, how to solo over it etc. With Lennie it was about improvising lines. The chords were there, but his emphasis was on the line itself. I was using fairly flat, vanilla-type chords. I did not learn the hip jazz chords (i.e. chords with extensions, other than the 7th) or passing chromatic chords – or as Attila would describe these, "the in-between shit". He would say, "Why are you playing these chords? That's corny shit!" I had to catch up. With Lennie, it was play the tune, and then improvise – the chromatic chords were superimposed in the line.

At the time I didn't feel that I could sit-in with the jazz guys. Attila however did invite me to join him on a tour of Germany. Before the trip I really got his tunes down. That was the time I was best at playing his stuff. I didn't play the big concert gigs but we played duo in some clubs and smaller venues. The upside for me was that I would get into the clubs for free with Attila, and I met some great musicians such as Ron Carter, Kenny Barron, and Jimmy Raney.

I was in jazz heaven: I felt like "King Shit!"

All in the Mind – Attila's Impact on Me

Attila was like a bull and could be very aggressive and sometimes intimidating. It was just his nature.

Attila knew the jazz language. But he didn't sit down and teach it to me. He would just get impatient with me and say, "Why are you playing like that?" As a result, I would feel very nervous about playing with him. If I am honest, Attila knocked me back. The more I played with him, the more insecure I got. And at that age, I didn't have the presence of mind to say "fuck that" and distance myself from it. I just didn't have the confidence as a musician to do my own thing.

In general, Attila didn't make me feel good about my playing. But on the other hand he liked it – which is paradoxical . I don't think Attila thought I was a good jazz player – he used to say, "You do your own shit." But I think that he liked the fact that my playing was different. I have never thought of myself as a classic jazz player anyway. I have tapes of playing with Attila, and at times my playing was right there with Attila's. But it was never straight ahead be-bop jazz that we played together at the restaurant gig I had with him for two years. The gig we had at the Julia Restaurant, on the upper west side of Manhattan was the most learning and most fun I have ever had on a gig – every Sunday night for two years.

Attila and I had this stormy relationship, and at the end, it was difficult to be around him. Musically it was just too intimidating. But we remained friends. I would still go with him to his house in Vermont and we would play a little. He did admit to liking my playing during those sessions – he would say, "Play me some of that cotton-pickin' shit." And so I would take off on a Davis tune or something similar, Blind Blake for example, and Attila would be like, "Crazy baby!" He was a funny, funny guy. So our relationship reflected something of the contradictory nature of the man. On the one hand, Attila could be a hard person to be around, and yet he was capable of acts of huge generosity, even within the same evening.

I think that the two-year engagement at the Julia Restaurant with Attila really taught me some valuable lessons about being a professional musician. If you are a freelancer, you will encounter musicians, club owners, and promoters who are difficult to deal with. And if you are not having a good time on a gig, it is up to you to find a way through the situation, to get yourself back to the place where you can enjoy the gig, or at least get something out of it. So hanging with Attila was a great lesson in how to survive – that was a large part of what Attila was about – just survival. And in Attila's case, it was often a case of survival in spite of himself!

Lessons from Attila's Music

Attila's Tunes

Attila was an incredible tunesmith. Some of his incredible songs are based on Hungarian folk melodies, some are original melodies, and others are lines based on standards. Many of his records feature him playing "free".

Attila came from the "Viennese tradition." He was trained formally on the classical violin, playing the music of Bartok, and performing in his early years in the cafes of Vienna. I think that his sense of melody came from that background. In that way, I don't think of Attila as being part of the US jazz tradition – he moved into the US out of that European tradition. (By European tradition I don't mean that he was part of the Django Reinhardt, Jazz Manouche tradition – that is something different). To me Attila's tunes are not swing tunes, they are not be-bop tunes. They are just Attila's tunes. No one has really recorded them. Yet...

Attila's compositions are very sculptured – they're very thought out. Listen to *Alicia's Lullaby, Zen Dipper, Peace Tune, Meant to Be, Waltz for Joy*.[31] He recorded 'The Birds and the Bees' with Herbie Hancock in the 1960s.[32] So they are old tunes. I went to one of his final gigs, just before he died. As he played all of his tunes I realized, "Wow! He has been playing these tunes for forty years." Then I thought, well here I am doing my gigs playing the same tunes for ten years, some of them. Until that point my reaction was usually along the lines of, "Ah, that's terrible – the same songs for all those years." But on this occasion, something changed, as a result of hearing Attila play his repertoire. It suddenly occurred to me: "Wait a minute, that's your body of work, that's what you do. What is wrong with playing the same song for ten years?"

I've kind of grown into that with my own material. Now I can play my piece 'Lisboa'[33] and enjoy it, whereas five years ago I was getting bored with it. I was stuck in the mode of thinking that I'm playing the same song. But now every time I play that tune, I am thinking that it is totally different. It feels good. Somehow I have turned a corner with it, but it's taken a long, long, time to turn that corner. It's like you get bored with practicing, you get bored with your sound, and it can feel stale. And then something else clicks. I think that was what the mindset was with Attila. He wrote *The Birds and the Bees* and he played it for forty years – the same tune, the same way, the same arrangement – and pretty much the same solo too. If you listen to his solos in the sixties and the solo on his record *Lasting Love*, they are very similar.

But he found something fresh and spontaneous each time he played it. Learning that it's your musical responsibility to find something new or interesting in a tune was a great lesson to learn. And when you are working with your own repertoire, it is up to you to find new ideas in an existing (even an old) theme, riff, or melody line. Attila's music is a great example of someone who managed to find something new in familiar material, of creating within a familiar tune or context.

He was strict, protective even, about his tunes. For his sixtieth birthday I arranged one of his songs, *Peace Tune*. I wrote out a four-part harmony choir to it. Just four voices, lyrics, no guitar: *Show us the way, help us to care…* and recorded it on a cassette tape. I planned to surprise him and present the cassette and the score for his birthday. He day came and there were about twenty people in his living room. At the very end of the tune there was a one melody note I changed to adapt the arrangement for one of the voices. So I put the cassette on the machine and he listened to it going, "Crazy yah, cool." You know he's very like, "Ah beautiful, ah very, very crazy people, a beautiful voice, that crazy chick." And he's listening, and we get to the end of the tape, and he suddenly recoils: "What? What? You changed my fucking melody!" He flipped out. He started yelling at me, "You changed my fucking melody. That's my melody. How dare you change anything?" He was dead serious. "How dare you change my melody? That's my song. You can't do that." He was pissed off. In a way he was right. I mean, I did change the melody a little bit at the end. He was so livid. I was so embarrassed. Right there in front of everybody, he just started screaming, "How dare you change my fucking melody, you cock-sucking motherfucker. Get out of my fucking house!" As bizarre as this was, the lesson was learned. Respect the melody!

We had crazy fights before. One time after getting home late from a gig, I was listening to my answer-phone machine. I heard Attila's voice, "Hey, Woody baby, where's my daughter Alicia?" Next message: "Woody baby, it's ten o'clock, Alicia's not home yet – where is she?" In the next message he is a little more agitated: "Woody, I know you're with Alicia. Where the fuck is my daughter?" And the message after this he starts to lose it: "I know you're with my fucking daughter. Where is my fucking daughter? She's not home yet, you motherfucker!" And then in the last message he's screaming down the phone: "You piece of shit, where the fuck…? You're no friend of mine. You motherfucking…" And he's screaming so hard it's distorted on the answer-phone. And I'm listening to all this at two in the morning and I'm thinking, "Oh my god." And the then there is a last message: "I'm so sorry. She came home. Everything is beautiful. Ciao, Woody baby..." Sometimes Attila scared the shit out of me.

Attila's Approach to Soloing and Improvising

It's funny, I played with Attila for all those years and I still find it difficult to describe his playing, his approach to soloing. Attila I think basically played off a melody and the chord changes. His whole harmonic concept, I could never quite figure it out. It's like he's playing off the chords, a lot of chromatic chords in there, but he doesn't do his solos. They're not like your typical Charlie Christian solos, Wes Montgomery solos. He's got his own harmonic language. It's very angular; it's different. His soloing style reflected who he was as a person; it's very aggressive.

Attila's solo lines were very jagged – but with chromatics on the top. I never related to that sound, it wasn't the classic Charlie Christian or Bud Powell sound – he didn't use the same inflected rhythms. There wasn't the smooth attack of the other be-bop players.

Free Music

Attila was not part of Lennie's scene, but both musicians were among the first musicians to record what is known as "free music", playing without any set structure, melody, rhythmic feel or harmonic track. Just in the moment, spontaneous... free.

Lennie's first free music recordings were the two sides *Intuition* and *Digression* which were cut in 25 December of 1949.[34] I think, Lennie's idea of playing free was just part of being a musician. He saw it as a way of feeling the time, feeling the music – a way of "not thinking" while you played. Playing free music was a way of opening up and expanding your improvisational skills by not being restricted by the chord changes or rhythmic feel of a tune. It was a way of "relaxing" into the music and getting rid of restrictions. He also saw playing free as a way to "enter" a tune – a preamble of spontaneously feeling how the song should be entered.

As to what Attila's motivation was for playing "free" was I am still not entirely sure. But then, 'free' music is not meant to be understood.

Retaining a "Child-like" Sensibility

I think that on some level when you are deeply absorbed in what you are doing you become childlike. It is that spontaneity and the magic of total focus on the thing that's in front of you that becomes the unthinking joy. Despite his grumpiness and sometimes frightening temper, Attila had that childlike quality about him right until the end of his life; he was excited about music and his playing. He was like a big kid.

After his gigs we would be sitting in his car listening to his solos on tape. And every so often, he would get all excited, listening to his own playing, "Check this out... crazy baby!" He would be getting off on his own playing. That's what I really remember about Attila – just hanging out with him, the fun times and the laughter. On a good day, there was no one better to be around. He was totally into his music, and when he had that singular focus, he was irrepressible.

I still aspire to try and retain that sense of pure joy when playing, just like Attila did so naturally. If you are going to enjoy something, such as if you are into playing jazz, or even just improvising, you really have to lose yourself in it. To allow yourself to do that is not easy, and to do it takes discipline. That's the irony. You can't do it by getting high and getting drunk, or just saying "I'm goin' to lose it." Paradoxically, the more disciplined you are, the more you can lose yourself and that's why these guys are so good at what they do. John Monteleone makes guitars with that total focus, Attila always practiced guitar with that same total focus, the same with Lennie.

They were always doing their thing in that total way. So sooner or later, as you are putting the time in, you can reach those moments of spontaneity. The key is staying in touch with the joy in what you are doing – and for some of us giving yourself permission to enjoy it – to sustain the journey.

Beware the Need for Recognition – The Perils of the Ego

Playing music is a very strange thing to do for a living because it's really hard to not let your ego get caught up in it. It's a real challenge to remain focused on the music when not only do you always ask yourself "Am I any good?" but also, "Am I getting the recognition I deserve?" The business end of music can be tough on one's ego. I suspect that a lot of the greats I have known isolated themselves, in part, for this reason. Lennie in his house in Queens, NY, and Jimmy D'Aquisto in his place further on Long Island. That was the downfall of Attila, his ego. Because he kept on thinking, "I'm not recognized," he would always get nervous about where his place was: "This motherfucker, I'm better than this guy." Attila could have had a fantastic career. When he played everybody loved him but he didn't have the ability to step back, put his ego aside, and as a result he wasn't able to make the most of the opportunities that came his way. He had the chance to be in the well-known jazz fusion band Weather Report but when co-leader/pianist and fellow Austrian Joe Zawinal called him to his office to ask him to talk about joining his group, Attila blew it. He listened to the rough tracks of their music and said to Joe Zawinal (as he told me), "This is shit – I can't play this shit..." Attila was just unable to take that final step.

At the core of it was that Attila, at least by the time I met him, has a very bitter side. This was, as far as I could tell, entirely down to the lack of recognition of his contribution, not just to the music, but also his innovations in the development of the instrument. He developed pick-ups for electric guitars (most notably he developed the Shadow AZ48 and AZ49 pick-ups which were manufactured by the Shadow company in Germany), guitar strings, even the instruments themselves. Basically he thought that everyone ripped him off. And in his apartment you had to be careful – if he lost his temper objects could literally fly across the room, and many times I heard him scream, "I was there first!" For example, if you happened to mention a particular manufacturer of guitar strings in his house, he would lose it and start throwing things. With Attila there was very little self-censorship – and you had to be careful.

My feeling was that the root of Attila's aggression was that he felt like an outsider. He was a European musician coming from a different tradition. He understood the jazz vocabulary, but he interpreted it in his own way. The result was a highly original style, a distinctive sound; he fused jazz with his eastern European, gypsy roots. Attila knew this, and I think that he was insecure about his place. The irony is that he was original and did not need to "fit in". And the funny thing was that the US musicians respected Attila. On balance, Attila's worst enemy was himself.

Even when I was working on his last record, I used to go to his house for dinner and he'd play his guitar. He'd pick up the guitar and play this beautiful, beautiful stuff and I'd say, "Attila that's gorgeous." You know, we'd be just sitting around on the couch and I'd say, "Attila you should record that." He just said, "No, nobody wants to hear that shit. What are you talking about? They want to hear modern, avant-garde stuff…" To him being a jazz guitar player was a kind of macho thing. Sometimes I got the feeling he wanted to prove himself because he wasn't an American, and that he thought somehow that he was seen as second class. "No-one wants to hear that slow shit, they want to hear that macho shit." I said, "No Attila, it's great." "No fuck that!" He never would record it until his last CD "Lasting Love".

"When It's Time" – Attila's Last Record

When Attila got sick with cancer, I told him he has to make a record of his solo compositions. For years he thought nobody would be interested, or it was not strong enough to record as a soloist. I'm not sure but I do know he was dead against it in the past. Finally now, he relented, "OK, I'll record it if you produce it." And I said "No way." Based on my past dealings I knew we'd get into a fight and it would be some crazy drama. But Peter Finger, the owner of Acoustic Music Records based in Germany was a good friend who respected Attila's work. I told him that Attila was not doing well and Peter said, "OK whatever you need, let's do it." I just said, "I'm not getting involved with the money," and once Attila and Peter hashed out the business end of things, I signed on to produce the record. I really needed to make it happen given that Attila's health was by that stage declining rapidly. It was going to be a race against time.

So we went into the studio but Attila wouldn't play. He would get very nervous when we went for a take and he knew he was being recorded. Take after take he would only get through one or two choruses before he stopped and got more frustrated. So Don Sternecker, the recording engineer and I would trick him. We'd say, "Attila we have to go out for a burger, you go practice." And we'd sneak behind him so he couldn't see us. We'd be lying on the floor of the studio and Don would hit the record button. Atilla was thinking he was just warming up. He was loose. I'd pop up and say "Great Attila, nice job." He would say, "What do you mean? Let's record it." I said, "No we have it, we've recorded it." "You recorded that shit? Crazy baby. Beautiful." It was a difficult session but also full of laughter.

I asked Jim Hall and Pat Metheny to write the sleeve notes to the CD. Both of them provided glowing quotes about Attila's record – a powerful endorsement of his music:

"An outstanding recording by an outstanding artist. A longtime friend and one of my favorite guitarists." (Jim Hall's notes to "Lasting Love")

"Attila Zoller has been and continues to be a major source of inspiration for me since he was my first serious guitar teacher back in 1968 when I was a fourteen year old student at a band camp in Central Illinois. With his first ever solo album, I am reminded of the uniqueness that Attila is able to channel the beauty and warmth of his spirit into a singular and unique guitar voice that has rightly earned him the respect and admiration of jazz fans worldwide over an expansive and rich 40 year career. Listening to the piece "The Birds and the Bees" (maybe one of Attila's most loved compositions) reminds me of the debt that I and so many other younger guitarists who have been influenced by Attila's unique harmonic and stylistic approach to the instrument owe him. Playing solo is one of the most difficult settings for any improvising guitarist, and on this record Attila meets the challenge by bringing the same individuality and joyful exuberance that has made him an important figure in the ongoing evolution of jazz guitar to the table. Attila is one of my main heroes!" (Pat Metheny's notes to "Lasting Love")

I had wonderful contributions for the sleeve notes from so many great musicians but I wasn't sure how Attila would respond since he could be touchy about how he related to other performers. This sense of caution stemmed from an incident that occurred when I was traveling in Europe with Attila. We were in Graz, Austria. It was the morning of a concert and we were sitting in a cafe drinking coffee and taking in the atmosphere of Austrian café society. Attila saw a flyer for the evening's concert on the table. He picked it up, read it, and he just lost it. The offending paragraph was the section where they described Attila as "a friend to Jim Hall, teacher to Pat Metheny." He took it as a slight because he felt he should be recognized in his own right, and not an attraction riding the coattails of other artists. "How dare they... they think I'm an old man, not famous enough! ... Come on, we're leaving..." he screamed. And he stormed off – we left town almost immediately and he just didn't show up at the gig.

So against the backdrop of this story, I was trying to deal with Peter to get the record out quickly. He sent me a sample of the CD sleeve and I thought, "Oh shit, if Attila sees Pat Metheny's quote on the CD cover, he's going to flip." Not only was I worried about his temper, I also didn't want to stress him because he was sick. I said, "Peter, we got to get this record down really fast. Attila's in the hospital, let's get it done." And Peter turned it around in two weeks and the record was shipped with Pat Metheny's notes on the back, together with Jim Hall's. I could have used dozens of people, but I just used those two and worried that Attila would flip. I took the CD to Attila, who was at that stage in hospital. He looked at it. I was a nervous wreck, thinking, "Ah, here we go." And I thought he would react badly: "You're no friend of mine, you motherfucker," that sort of thing.

We had all these fights in the past, all that history. But he looked at the record and he goes, "Ah beautiful, crazy baby." And he listened to the record: "This is the best record I ever did." And for weeks he's walking around saying "This is my record. I should have done this record thirty years ago. This is the best fucking shit I've ever played in my life." And he was just over the top. He was so thankful. It was really a great thing to witness him being just so happy. And I was so scared he'd be flipping out. What an experience.

This record is really something great. Don Sternecker, the master the sound engineer with whom I have worked for years on my own recordings, did an amazing job recording it. And best of all, Attila loved it: "Best shit I've ever played in my life." We just got it down in time because – he was just losing strength. In another few weeks he couldn't have recorded any more. It was a deeply rewarding experience and something I am very proud of.

Beyond the Enigma

Finishing his last record and getting it shipped to him just before he died was a poignant moment. As to whether this record represented some sort of resolution for Attila at the end of his life, it is hard to tell. Ultimately what I remember about Attila is the person I saw when he held complete and total focus on his music – that pure joy he found in his music. At those times his enthusiasm was infectious. Above all though, I am grateful that he took me under his wing – at times he showed me incredible generosity. At his core, I know that he was a kind person with a big heart – and for me this feeling is what the brilliant compositions he left us ultimately express. That I am sure is what will endure as far as Attila is concerned. Thankfully he did leave us with a recorded legacy so that in the future younger players can discover his music and his musicianship.

Atilla

Chapter 5

Carlos Paredes – A Mirror of Sounds

During the 1990s I was married to Teresa, who was Portuguese. She had a cassette tape of this guy playing his own music, not on a regular steel stringed guitar, but a Portuguese guitar. I asked her, "What is that?" I had never heard anything like it. I had no idea what a Portuguese guitar was, but when I heard the music, I just fell in love with it and was totally mesmerized. It turns out that the guitar player who had captured my attention was Carlos Paredes. I don't know how to define the word 'genius' – it isn't a word that I use lightly – but it felt like I was hearing one. His music just revealed itself through the speaker of my old cassette deck, completely original and with his own rich musical vocabulary. It seemed to me that his sensibility was uniquely Portuguese, and yet his music didn't seem to be based directly on any particular musical tradition, such traditional Fado music or even western classical music. Even his instrument of choice was unknown to me. Before the revelation of hearing Paredes' music for the first time I didn't know anything about the Portuguese guitar.

The Guitarra Portuguesa

The Portuguese guitar is different from the Spanish guitar that most people are familiar with. It is smaller and is strung with six courses of two strings each – basically a 12-string guitar. The modern Portuguese guitar has two variants, the guitar of Lisboa and the guitar of Coimbra. The Lisboa guitar is slightly smaller, has a slightly shorter scale length and is usually tuned a whole step higher than the Coimbra guitar. By comparison the Coimbra guitar is the plainer looking instrument with fewer adornments. It is the Coimbra guitar that was the chosen instrument of the Paredes dynasty, hailing as they did from Coimbra. The Coimbra guitar itself closely resembles the so-called 'English Guitar,' a type of cittern that had been modified by English, Scottish, Dutch and German luthiers, and introduced into Portugal (specifically the northern city of Oporto through the trading connections between that city and the cities of northern Europe) in or around 1750.[35] In the rest of Europe the Spanish Guitar rose to prominence and older instruments such as the cittern and the English guitar gradually became obsolete. In Portugal however, these instruments underwent a process of further development and refinement, resulting in the two variants of the Portuguese guitar known to us today. Typically the Portuguese guitar is accompanied by a second guitar, basically a steel stringed guitar tuned slightly lower than usual called a *viola* in Portuguese.

The sound of the Guitarra Portuguesa is more delicate than a normal steel string guitar. I imagine the instrument as a sort of 12 string mandolin with the warmth of a harp. It has 12 strings, six courses of two strings each with each pair of strings tuned in octaves, rather like a 12 string guitar. But the tuning across the courses of strings has different intervals, for example major 2nds, and a completely different sonority. The basic tuning is C G A D G A - this is the Coimbra guitar tuning – the Lisboa model has the same interval relationships but one step higher.

A Mirror of Sounds

"*Espelho de sons*"[36] – translated from the Portuguese it means, roughly, "mirror of sounds." It is also the name Carlos Paredes gave to one of his records. What a fantastic idea – a sound recording as a "mirror of sounds." It accurately sums up much of what Carlos Paredes' guitar playing represents. He viewed that record as:

"... a mirror with which the hands of guitarists have created the sounds and images of the things we love. It has been thus, from one generation to the next, that the distinctive and special forms of Portuguese guitar playing have developed. The pieces of music in this recording have been selected in keeping with this ideal, with the intention of creating in the imagination of the listener the reflections and images of the sights and sounds of Portugal."[87]

And further:

"The linking of the abstract quality of the sound produced by the guitarist, and the evocation of specific images in the imagination of the listener has always been an integral part of the mystique of the Portuguese guitar."

To my ears Paredes' music is a mixture of European and Moorish sounds. It is diatonic music, but his sensibility, his phrasing and the melodies are uniquely Portuguese. His music affected everybody, from every social and economic strata, and yet it's not folk music, it's not classical music, it's not vocal music. It's really extraordinary when you think about how his music touched people. It resonates with a deep feeling of connection. For example, in compositions like *Dança dos Montanhas (Dance of the Mountains)* you can almost see the mountains and experience directly the evocativeness of it all.

Carlos Paredes' music is little known in the US, or anywhere outside his native Portugal where he is revered, not only for his virtuosity on the guitarra Portuguesa, his main instrument, but also for what he represents as a former political prisoner under the Salazar regime.

From the Edge of Europe

Carlos Paredes was born in 1925 into a musical family. His father was Artur Paredes, another virtuoso of the Portuguese guitar (born 10 May 1899, died 20 December 1980). His grandfather was Goncalo Paredes, also a highly regarded Portuguese guitarist. All generations of his family spawned great composers. Goncalo Paredes wrote Variations on the "Ballade de Mondego."[38] His son, Artur, wrote several variations on this piece – and Carlos recorded their variations on several occasions.[39] A dynasty of great musicians.

The Paredes family moved from Coimbra to Lisbon in 1931, where Carlos would remain for the rest of his life. He started working at the Hospital of St Joseph (Sao Jose Hospital) in its x-ray archive department in 1949 where he worked as a civil servant. During the 1950s and 1960s, Paredes was a member of the Portugese Communist Party and as a result of his opposition to the Salazar dictatorship, was imprisoned by the PIDE (the "Policia Internacionale de Defesa do Estado" or International and State Defence Police) in 1958. Some of his time as a prisoner was spent in solitary confinement – and there is the story that he walked around his cell pretending to play music, which naturally led some of the inmates at the prison to believe that he was insane. In fact he was apparently composing music in his mind. He was eventually released from prison after 18 months in 1960. Upon his release he was expelled from the Portuguese Civil Service, only to be re-instated at the hospital following the October 1974 revolution in Portugal. He remained at the hospital until he retired in 1986. Following the revolution (known as the Carnation Revolution because the soldiers apparently placed carnations in the ends of their firearms), Paredes, along with the other political prisoners, was hailed as a hero. An unassuming man, Paredes never believed himself to be special, and is said to have commented only that "many people have suffered worse than I."

However, while his professional career was sketchy in terms of continually touring and concertizing, Paredes still had an audience.

Like Rev. Davis and Lennie, he still cut his teeth as a musician performing in public. In terms of his output, Paredes wrote music for the theatre, scores for cinematic films, traditional puppet theatre, the Gulkenbian Ballet of Lisboa. His range was far wider than simply recording 'guitar music,' great though his music is when you just listen to it as such.

Another Telephone Call...

I first traveled to Portugal in the early 1990s. On that trip I remember one day with Teresa's family, I said, "I want to meet Carlos Paredes." They were shocked: "You're crazy, you can't meet him." "Why not?" I retorted. It was because he was one of the most beloved icons of Portugal. I didn't know about his story, how before the 1974 revolution in Portugal, he had been branded as a communist and imprisoned by the Salazar regime. So, the man and his music represents for many Portuguese, freedom. He was one of the most famous figures of the revolution. Teresa's family just said, "You can't meet him." To the Portuguese it was like, "Oh, he's too famous. He's not one of us." I said, "What are you talking about? I just want to meet the guy." They were like, "Oh! We don't know anybody who knows him." Her family was just impossible. It was like I was asking them if I could meet the President.

I'll never forget the occasion. They were gathered in the kitchen. I went to the living room – and this had shades of Gary Davis – I went to the telephone book. Remember that I'm in Portugal and I don't even speak the language. All the same, I went through the 'phone book and looked up Paredes – P-A- R-E-D-E-S – and I dialed the number. I just called him up. Of course there was more than one 'Carlos Paredes' in the Portuguese telephone book, but I finally called this one number up and Luisa, his wife, answered the telephone. It was just like when Annie answered the telephone with Rev. Davis. I asked, "Is this the home of Carlos Paredes, the famous guitar player?" She replied, "Yeah." I said, "My name is Woody. I'm from

New York and I'm over here and I love his music and I was just wondering..." Thankfully Luisa spoke good English. I just blurted it out: "I wonder if I can come over and meet him?" And she said "Yeah, come on over tomorrow." It's a funny parallel to how I first met Davis at his house for a lesson – how I met two of the most important people and greatest musicians I ever met.

Having made arrangements to visit Carlos, I went back to the kitchen. I told the family "Oh by the way, I just talked to Luisa, Carlos Paredes' wife, and I'm going there tomorrow." And they flipped but not before finding out if it was really true: "No! You're bullshitting," to which I said "I've just come off the telephone with her." I gave them the address, Avenue de Uruguay, and they started calling all their friends and relatives: "You won't believe what Woody did. The New Yorker showed up here and..." All the neighbors knew, *everybody* knew. When I went down to the local café they asked me, "What, did you call Carlos Paredes?" I was the subject of a lot of gossip: "He's going to meet Carlos Paredes!" It was this huge, huge thing. The next day there was a crowd at the cafe watching us depart in three cars to Carlos' house. It was hysterical. Anyway, we went there and had a good time, it was powerful and magical. I had heard his recordings of course, but hearing the power of his sound and seeing the ease and joy of his playing was profound. He was at one with it all; the music, the instrument, the expression. I just watched him play and asked him some questions. He did not speak English but somehow we communicated. Luisa, his wife, interpreted our conversation. Her professional name is Luisa Amaro and she is an incredibly talented Guitarra Portuguessa player and performer in her own right. She played the viola (guitar) on many of Carlos' recordings. He was gracious and asked me to play for him. It was a blur. I was in awe and wanted to learn more about his music. I tried to play one of his guitars but it was too difficult. He used heavy strings coupled with a high action. This made his instruments very loud with a grand tone, but with a really hard touch. I couldn't even finger single notes let alone chords. Through friends I met another guy, Alexandre Battiera's who played his music, and I did take a few lessons from him. Alexandre played all of Carlos's music but he wasn't a professional musician or well known in Portugal. So as I watched him play, it was like "Ah, that's how you do it!" So I got a lot from him. From there it was an easier jump towards learning directly from Carlos' recordings.

During one of the visits to his apartment, he and Luisa invited me out to dinner to his favorite restaurant. He knew the chef and he had special food prepared for him. It was a very special time. It was at the restaurant where he explained to me what it was like living under the Salazar regime, how they couldn't gather more than three people in one place. He described how he had a meeting at the restaurant and as his friends left, Salazar's people gunned them down right in front of the restaurant, killed where we were now sitting. And he explained the underground. Evidently there were supposedly some underground passages in Lisbon that people just disappeared into, and that Salazar had this network of tunnels that led to some kind of Gulag. People just disappeared. They weren't allowed to gather in groups of more than three or four people. Any time a group gathered the police would come in and break it up. And after the revolution, cafés opened up because people could gather. It's the first time they could get, like, ten people together and sit in a café.

"The Well" – Where Does it Come From?

Paredes is often described, at least in English language sources as a Fado musician. It is true that he could play it and was associated with the great Fado singer Amalia Rodrigues, Fado music's most accomplished exponent. But that label doesn't really capture the full breadth of Paredes' musicianship or his achievements as a composer. His music is definitely roots music – it's from a tradition; there is a sense that it's uniquely Portuguese. Yet it's not based on a Portuguese folk music tradition. There's no genus of a folk form or even just a melody, that he took and contemporized. He was completely original and although coming from a small tradition of solo guitar, changed the course of the instrument. It was like Charlie Parker in jazz being the pivotal figure – similar to how jazz music is often divided up into "pre-Bird" and "post-Bird" jazz.

What amazes me is his creativity – the ability that he had to capture that essence of place and to express it so vividly in music. The feel, rhythm, phrasing, approach, and Portuguese sensibility shines through, and yet he created a new musical language for the Portuguese guitar. That ability to be at once an innovator and also conservative in his reverence for place, tradition, the Portuguese way, is a rare quality. And yet, he made his living as a hospital worker... just incredible.

The main influences you hear in Carlos Paredes' music, at least to my ears, are from his father, Artur Paredes or perhaps from the virtuoso of the "Lisboa" guitar, Armandhino.[40] You can hear that in the records. You can tell there's a virtuoso aspect to the Portuguese guitar. The techniques he used later were so obviously learned from his father and from Armandhino's records. But he also took it a step further with his own music, in terms of expressiveness, the creativity. Carlos' music was so much more lyrical in the melodies, phrasing and touch. He wasn't just this random creative musician who just had this conceptual sense of playing whatever. It is very steady, the rhythm is exact, and with a very thought-through, high level of technique, speed and accuracy, sound, vibrato. Completely original and unbelievable technique. Passionate. It's amazing stuff.

Another Way to be Creative – His Musical Palette

Unlike Lennie and Attila, Carlos Paredes was not really an improvising musician – at least not in the jazz sense or even the sense in which Davis improvised within the forms that were familiar to him as "part of his bag." When Paredes played, nothing was really left to chance. For example, he was very strict with his second guitar parts. He was a taskmaster. When it came to phrasing, the guitar part had to be exact. I mean everything was really, really rehearsed. Luisa told me that when they worked out the guitar parts for their duets it was very strict. He knew exactly how it would go, the dynamics, the "boom-ching" feel. Nothing was left to chance. So he definitely had a concept of what it should sound like.

With Paredes I get more of a sense that he had a singular vision of music, which seems to have allowed him to dig deeper into his own sound to develop a unique voice on the guitar. However his music isn't part of a tradition in the jazz sense, so the requirement of being able to interact with other musicians, as a jazz musician needs to, is sort of suspended in Paredes' case.

He could and did, on occasion, improvise. On his records you hear he does play some free improvisation. But his compositions, what he is really well known for, are set and tightly arranged. If you listen to some of the compositions on different albums he plays them differently: slower or faster. So to me, there's definitely *some* improvisational sense to his music. When you hear *Os Verdes Anos*, there are ten different recordings, all really different. It's the same song, but very different. Not just tempo wise. There's a whole middle section in one. The tune becomes a different thing on each recording. They are sort of arrangements, if you like, or developments of variations on the theme. He had his set of songs, his repertoire. Look how many years he played *Os Verde Anos* and *Canto de Amor* and all of his songs. He played the same basic repertoire for thirty years, forty years, fifty years.

When you hear his records, most of them contain the same songs, which is really interesting. Here's a guy that made fifteen albums. And pretty much on every record there's going to be those tunes, or at least a new variation on those same tunes. And if you think about that idea, nobody does that. I mean, what artist (other than a jazz musician) records five different takes of the same song?

The variations he created for his own compositions over a period of decades reflected his huge imagination. Paredes' music is also an example of how to create new and original music out of a tradition (even if it is the 'tradition' as it was developed out of the innovations of your own father and grandfather).

It is remarkable that he grew up under the influence of his father's playing, and yet managed to forge his own unique body of work, his own sound and touch on the guitar. He absorbed their influence, often paid homage to their music, yet he managed to break free from it. Paredes achieved artistic independence from them. I am still not sure exactly how he broke free from his father's influence or what drove him to do so. Was it his own ego that pushed him to forge his own identity as a musician, or was it a competitive conflict with his father? It was a strange mixture of modesty with a drive to emulate or even surpass the achievements of his father. I didn't get to spend enough time with him to ask him where his drive to create such an original body of music came from.

Paredes' music is so different than that of Gary Davis, Lennie or Attila. There is little or no musical language in common and it is hard to identify a common cultural reference point between them. And yet, they all created incredible guitar music. Further, Davis, Lennie, Attila and Carlos were singular artists who did not spawn a "school" of guitar players who imitated them. For me personally, there is an intrinsic honesty to their music, which reflected who they were as people, and that is what connects them. They each had that quality of mastery.

I think Paredes established the Portuguese guitar as a solo art form, a solo tradition. He opened the door for people to learn the tradition, but they didn't necessarily play his songs. And yet, at that time, none of his music was written down, none of it.

Unfinished Business

I remember running into Carlos on the streets in Lisbon a few years later. I recognized him and went up to him and said "Carlos, remember me?" And he was a little lost. He was standing on the street in downtown Lisbon and I said "Are you OK?" He was just kind of smiling. I asked him if I could get anything for him. He was dazed and lost. And I remember we got him a taxi because it looked like he was trying to hail a taxi. It looked like he was just wandering, and I think that's around the time when he started losing it. He went into the hospital shortly after that. But he was just standing on the corner, smiling. He seemed dazed and confused. I don't think he knew where he was. I helped him get into a taxi and told the driver his address. That was the last time I saw him. I heard that despite his ill health, he managed to perform his music up until the very end.

For a time during the late 1990s I was the only member of the New York Musicians Union who listed the Guitarra Portuguesa as an instrument. I got a call asking me to play the score of a film on the Portuguese guitar, which I accepted enthusiastically as a new challenge. I jumped at the opportunity to try something different; and this was something that fascinated me and gripped my attention. I remember little or nothing of the actual recording sessions. In the end they ran smoothly. The drama took place in my lead up and preparation for the record date – the difficulties I had in getting the music down on the Portuguese guitar and the resulting sleeplessness I experienced in the week before going into the studio. In the end the obstacles were overcome and the recordings were successful.

Around the same time was invited to play a concert on the Guitarra at Portugal World Expo in Lisbon. The theme of the concert series was how musicians from various countries and musical backgrounds interpreted the instrument. I had no repertoire, original or otherwise. It was one of the most nerve-wracking experiences, especially since I was playing for a mostly Portuguese audience! Needless to say, I worked my ass off developing a set of music and spent many a day in the stairwell developing ideas.

It was a joy and a great creative experience to discover the possibilities of the instrument and how personal it felt to me. When, at the Expo concert, I mentioned Carlos' name as my inspiration, the audience stood up and cheered – not for me but for him. There was just such reverence for this guy.

In retrospect, it is a shame that I didn't build further on this project. I had the momentum at that time and I felt I could have nailed the Guitarra Portuguesa. I remember John Pearse said "You should do a Portuguese guitar recording project," and it's something I regret not doing when I was really into it. I did record about six Carlos Paredes tunes with Nik Munson, who played the guitar and bass parts, but we didn't release it. I should have built on that – unfinished business indeed.

Carlos Paredes

Chapter 6

Just Play

"You're a musician. You've played since you were a kid. You play because you love it. I can hear it. You love it. That's why you play. And that's the reason you play... the reason you play is because you love it. That's you."

These are the words that Lennie Tristano spoke to me when I was in my early 20s. They are etched into my mind permanently – simple, direct and bang on the money. If there is a single word which best describes what Lennie Tristano's approach to music is all about, it is "play." Lennie's "just play" approach to music has been something that I always shoot for: taking the thinking mind out of the process. It is a simple idea to grasp but for some of us, it is a difficult thing to do. It also means taking the "thinking mind" out of the process of making music – not as a short cut, but a way of making a direct connection with the "feeling" of your music. When I fall into the trap of over analyzing my music I always go back to the very basics to calm it down – just as Lennie used to suggest.

The idea of "play" gets us to the heart of their music. It reveals its true value to musicians, whatever genre or style of music they are working in. Certainly neither Lennie nor Davis ascribed any mystical value to what they were doing and were, as teachers, concerned with setting out their approach clearly. If anything, their approaches were very "matter of fact," very direct. At times, blunt even. I remember Lennie on many occasions would say, "There isn't anything special about me – I'm just a wop piano player – If I can do it so can you" hardly the words of someone wishing to do that academic thing of inventing their own peculiar terminology, so that their field of study is unintelligible to the rest of humanity.

It is an activity that Lennie, Attila, and Carlos pursued with incredible focus and which when combined with highly developed musical skills, allowed them to tap into "the flow". The same applies to other artists and performers who apparently only played for financial reward, and who gave up playing once there was no living to be gained from doing so. In my experience, the legendary blues singer and bottleneck guitarist Son House is a perfect example of this. When he couldn't earn enough money by performing music, he simply stopped playing – but when he was playing, even as an older man with severe health issues, he was completely committed – he tapped into this flow and delivered some of the most powerful performances I ever witnessed.

You might say that their musicianship is a form of "deep play."[41] It is a heightened experience; something exhilarating. It has no objective, no end, no 'learning outcome' – you might even say it has no 'point.' It is an experience that is intrinsically rewarding – and that's it.

The justification of music is music. The art of playing your instrument justifies music. The point is to recognize that when you are playing, you are in a certain place or state, or a flow, and that the purpose of that flow is to keep on flowing. As I remember Lennie always saying to me:

"Listen, you play music because you love it, get in touch with that."

To answer the question, "why do we play music?" – it really is simple. There is a sound that at some point in our lives captures our attention, and then keeps on capturing our attention. Because it makes us feel good. And then Lennie would say:

"How much can you dig, can you really enjoy it, can you really take it?"

He kept saying: "How much can you take? Can you take the joy?" It was like a mantra. And his point is that we play music because we enjoy it; it is that feeling which is at the heart of it.

It's that balance, and that's the art of practicing, the art of playing and the art of living; to maintain that curiosity, the spontaneity and the joy.

Chapter 7

How It All Connects...

The Enduring Relevance of My Lessons

The lessons that I learned from Davis, Lennie, Attila and Paredes have become "hard wired" into my thinking. My lessons were not "once and for all" lessons – they were much more dynamic than that. They also became a framework for living.

When I think about what common ground these artists share in their approaches to their art the one thing that stands out; the simplicity of it. They all explained it in a very basic way. Like the way it was with Lennie: "Fuck, just play!" It was the same with Jimmy D'Aquisto, "I don't know, it's a piece of wood!" John: "I don't know, I just built it that way". Even when I was with Carlos Paredes, he didn't speak a word of English. I couldn't understand him when he tried. But his approach was to just work every nuance of a melody and rhythm – keeping it simple. They explained what they did as a craft. I understood that clearly enough. Attila, I mean, he was just totally nuts, in a beautiful way.

Getting good at your chosen instrument (and hopefully mastering it) is really about the art of practicing. There is no mystery. All you really need to do is learn a couple of tunes – as was Lennie's credo:

"You can learn more from penetrating the form of one tune than you can by merely "memorizing" many tunes... through deep immersion in that one tune, you will evolve to another level of playing." [42]

It is easy to fall into the habit of trying run before you can walk, trying to learn too much at once. The conversation quickly becomes about trying to cut corners: "What's that secret riff? What's that chord progression? What's that two-five-one chromatic cool thing?" In trying to cut the corners we rush through the material, trying to get to the end of it but not managing to internalize it. It is an old conversation for me, which Kenny Werner captures perfectly:

"You see, fear has ruined your practicing by rushing through the material, rendering you unable to absorb anything. You try to cover too much ground every time you practice, barely skimming the surface of each item, and then moving on. You ignore the fact that you can barely execute the material, because you have no time to notice that. After all, there's so much to practice and so little time! It's frustrating – even though you are practicing all this stuff, your playing is not improving much. Nothing is mastered." [43]

Take it slowly and find the joy in playing a piece of music simply. Even better, take the time to play an exercise as if it were a piece of music. It is about finding the music and the enjoyment in our practicing and learning – finding the joy in what you are doing. Lennie says it beautifully:

"The music is already in your head – and all you do is let your hands, depending on what instrument you play, reproduce what you hear as you hear it. So what you come up with is something completely spontaneous. Like when you hear a great Charlie Parker solo what you actually do is experience somebody in the act of creating beauty."

Taking lessons and learning is an on-going process. Of course, nobody develops in exactly the same way or at the same speed, and in a way that doesn't matter. What's important is just staying engaged with the idea of learning. It is about building up that complex set of nuances, including staying receptive to learning new things so that they becomes part of the fabric of how you live.

Finding Equilibrium: Teaching and Performing... (and Writing and Producing...)

Teaching and performing appear to be different things, separate activities. But for me they are both about breaking down the music, keeping it simple. Both activities stem from working towards trying to master the craft of music. In that way they are part of the same thing. When I write an instruction book, it is not just about teaching the reader a new repertoire (although that is important). I also hope that my books offer something further, a road map perhaps into how they can understand the music, whether it is a simple ragtime piece, blues or jazz.

Most of my projects have been born out of the co-existence of teaching and performing. They feed into each other – the one activity enriches the other and vice versa. This creates creative energy – the possibility that something new is just around the corner. The symbiosis between teaching and performing has had an impact on my career that I could not have foreseen. How could I have known that writing one book when I was still a teenager would lead to a new career direction opening up more than twenty years later?

In 1972 I wrote a book, *Six Early Blues Guitarists*[44] – I was 18 years old at the time. I had no idea back then that the book would have such a long shelf life. It is not that this book sold many copies – it never was a bestseller. What was important though is that this book took on a life of its own and has been distributed in parts of the world that I only got to visit myself several decades later. It is curious to me that this book had a reach far beyond that which I ever anticipated when

I wrote it. The book came about because I knew Nick Perls. He knew a publisher who was looking to write a blues guitar instruction book and Nick recommended me. The project quickly became a collaborative effort with Steve Calt: I transcribed the music and Steve wrote the biographies for the musicians. It was a very exciting project for me – my first book. I just happened to be in the right place, at the right time and possessed the right combination of skill sets required to write a transcription book about blues musicians.

Moving forward twenty years to when blues music became popular again in the early 1990s, I took a call from Liverpool, England. On the other end of the telephone line was Brendan McCormack, a well-known English musician.[45] Brendan explained that he was setting up a new festival in the UK, the International Guitar Festival of Great Britain. The festival was to be held in Birkenhead, which is situated on a peninsula of Northwest England known as the Wirral. Birkenhead itself is found on the opposite side of the River Mersey to the City of Liverpool. Brendan asked me to play at his festival and also to teach a guitar workshop the following day. At that time I did not have a solo acoustic set. But I took the gig anyway and then thought, "What am I going to play?" I had to pull back the old blues tunes that I had forgotten, and from there I started to piece it back together. I have returned to play at the Birkenhead festival ever since – it has been my regular gig for nearly 25 years – I am proud to be the official festival ambassador from the USA – and all off the back of writing a guitar instruction book. It could just be serendipity, but more likely because I had spent the previous twenty years combining many activities in order to make a living. Just working this way meant that I created a number of avenues through which promoters, event organizers and administrators could find me, and hopefully hire me.

How to Survive

I do not make my entire living by performing. Davis, Lennie, Attila all struggled throughout their lives. Lennie would always tell me to get a "real" job, get off at five and do my music after hours. He saw too many artists fail and his whole trip was to take care of yourself (put food on the table, clothe and shelter yourself) and I also saw Attila, as great a musician as he was, become bitter towards the end of his life. For me it was teaching, writing, and producing and film projects that I cultivated in addition to performing.

When I started out playing the guitar, teaching soon became a natural part of my musical work. In high school teaching the guitar to other students was a way of earning some extra pocket money. It became a natural outreach of my own learning because I had to explain the music to my students and figure out how it all worked. And performing extended from that because when you are teaching, you are also performing to a student. You are on the spot: you have to play the tune for them. It is a one to one performing situation, and you have to learn to deal with the same nerves that you get when you are performing to an audience. For me at least, the two have also grown together. The teaching progressed from giving one to one lessons during my high school years, to being asked to teach in local schools, and then I got a job teaching guitar at a few local guitar workshops, then universities and colleges, and at various guitar camps and seminars.

I have taught everyone from children to nuns, amateurs to professionals, talented and musically challenged people – all sorts. Teaching socializes you, and from that you become a better freelancer. So in that way too, teaching has helped me to manage my career as a performer – how to get along with people out on the road, dealing with all sorts of club owners, agents, promoters and assholes. My teaching activities culminated in taking on one of the biggest projects I have ever undertaken – in three letters: I-G-S...

International Guitar Seminars

As a teacher, one of the projects I am most proud of is the series of guitar workshops which Trevor Laurence and I ran from 1999 through to 2006 – International Guitar Seminars, or IGS at it became known amongst our students. Trevor is a gifted writer, director and film editor (and a pretty great guitarist as well). Soon after he started talking guitar lessons we became good friends and eventual business partners. I set up IGS as a vehicle through which I could continue to earn a living by teaching music. The idea was also to try something new, a fresh format, to work within a community and keep my teaching and the music invigorated. I cannot express the ethos and credo of IGS any better than how we set out the aims of the seminars in our original brochure:

"International Guitar Seminars is an intensive musical study program where participants come from all over the world to create an international community of musicians, all living together and sharing the learning experience. The non- competitive atmosphere and well balanced program provide students with the perfect setting for learning new styles, taking chances, and interacting with other musicians.

Our approach is to use the techniques of the traditional music masters as a "jumping off point" for further musical exploration – to develop your "toolbox" of expression. Our focused program explores the broad spectrum of acoustic blues, swing, slide and world music, as well as related genres such as Hawaiian slack key, ragtime & gospel, and jazz. The program is designed to give students the practical skills for jamming and performing and to offer new music perspectives that will last long after the week is over.

Through our travels as performers we continually meet guitarists who are looking for a sense of direction and a fresh input of ideas and repertoire in their playing. We realized that there was a need to create a "safe" place where beginners as well as advanced players can learn from each other, expand their musicianship, and take musical chances."

IGS expressed the values of all my great teachers but the ethos was really Lennie's. It was important to me that the teaching environment should be ego-free and honest: a safe space to allow students to focus on making music for music's sake. At the very least the seminars gave students an insight into what they could achieve in an environment conducive to working on the craft of their music – breaking down the music and getting deeper into it. For one week the students could experience total immersion in their music. IGS gave them a glimpse of their potential as musicians.

The idea was that we would cover all styles of acoustic roots music and hire a number of ancillary teachers who would act as musical instigators and plug any gaps. We hired the best musicians who also had the skill to teach. We would provide an intensive week of musical activity – not like a summer camp – more like a seminar. The sessions would be inclusive, not competitive – and that principle was sacrosanct throughout the lifespan of IGS.

And it was a great success. My core students were the people I met from touring Europe and Japan and teaching at other workshops. Despite the fact that, at that time, IGS was a brand new event with no history or proven track record, they made the effort to travel to the US and trusted that the seminars would be a success. I was flattered. We were never the cheapest music camp in the market place but we attracted all sorts of students; people getting back into their passion for music, professionals & amateurs. At the start of the week students would show up, not knowing quite what to expect and understandably nervous, not confident about their playing. So the first day or two of each session was really about everybody getting to know each other. Then, in addition to the morning seminar sessions, we would introduce ideas such as the "deconstructed jam" session, usually on day three, to make the idea of playing together in an ad-hoc group accessible, and then we would watch people realize "I can do this" and the week would just take off at that point. The walls came tumbling down and the students just opened up. By the end of the week, some students would get so enthusiastic that they would say, "I'm quitting my job!" Curiously I would find myself playing the "Mr Sensible" role: "Now don't make any life decisions for at least a week when you get home..." – I could hardly believe that I heard myself say it. Advice on life decisions from a working musician – seriously? But I think this points to what IGS was all about; it got people thinking about music in new ways, and most important, they got in touch with themselves and became receptive to new possibilities. That for me was the success of IGS. Yes, we balanced the books, we put on an organized and well-run event, but it was the fact that many students found the IGS experience to be life changing – that is what gave me the feeling that we achieved something positive with IGS.

But the changes that took place with our students weren't just personal. The community that developed during the IGS sessions took on a life of its own long after the jams had finished. The discussion forum on the IGS website existed as a virtual community which had its own dynamic – it even developed its own etiquette and form of self-regulation. We didn't plan it that way – it was the participants who shaped it – the forum became whatever it was they wanted it to become. There was a definite sense that people felt they belonged to that community. That is why the forum ran for nearly 10 years after the last IGS workshop was held. The IGS website made that connection between the teachers, and the hundreds (thousands) of guitar players out there, from all over the globe.

Continuing to Transmit the Message – Berklee

I have been an adjunct faculty member at a few music schools including Bard College and The Guitar Study Center at the New School in NYC where I taught private lessons, classes in blues, jazz, and theory. Recently I started teaching at Berklee College of Music in Boston as a visiting artist in a special country blues program, under the umbrella of their Roots Music department. It is endowed by Robert Davoli and Eileen McDonagh: *The Robert*

Davoli and Eileen McDonagh Country Blues Visiting Artist Program. It is the first program of its type in the USA.

Robert and Eileen are close friends. Family really. I first met Robert at the Seattle IGS session and our friendship grew from there. He is an artist, songwriter, and musician, as well as a successful businessman. Eileen is a prolific writer and scholar who has developed pioneering theories in the field of political science. Robert and Eileen understand that country blues, like jazz, is a vital part of American musical landscape and has been a musical tradition neglected in college-level music programs. It was their vision to inaugurate a country blues program at Berklee College of Music. Berklee embraces new ideas and understands that music styles and history are not engraved in stone. For me, the program allows my teaching, my research, and my love of playing to come together. Being asked to be part of this program as country blues visiting artist is truly a gift. Working with such talented students is a joy, and to see how they incorporate the craft of country blues into their own contemporary music and imbue it with a sense of roots is very exciting. Thrilling really. There are few people who can teach the history and play the music. I feel like I'm in the right place.

Here is something I wrote when I started teaching at Berklee.

American Roots: The Art of Country Blues

Country Blues...Why study it?

Country blues is an essential part of America's musical history. It is an art form that transcends its original times, offering a lasting body of material, techniques, and approaches to improvisation. Though its heyday in the 1920s and 30s is a distant memory for most musicians today, time has not diminished the musical contribution of the early masters. The instrumental, vocal and songwriting techniques, as well as their approaches to improvisation, were central to the development of America's roots music as well as the early jazz styles.

Historically, country blues traditions developed from the collective work of individual musicians. In the 1920s, itinerant musicians traveled throughout the South and Midwest playing on street corners, at local dances, and in churches. Their music was a confluence of sounds from African chants to the pop music of the day to Appalachian and English folk ballads. There was no one geographic center where musicians would meet. As a result, each artist developed his or her own sound, repertoire, and technique. In addition, jobs were scarce and highly competitive, encouraging little collaboration among musicians. The result was a genre rich in sounds and approaches defined by the individuality of the artists.

Today, country blues is often overlooked as a type of music that existed in a contained time and space. Though it's initial audience is gone, it is a genre that should not be simply acknowledged, but expanded. The instrumental and songwriting techniques as well as the approaches to improvisation are central to the development of America's roots music. It represents the beginnings of the jazz story and precursor to the early styles of King Oliver, Louis Armstrong, and the musicians who recorded in New Orleans in the late 1920s. Though its initial audience is gone, it is a genre that should not be simply acknowledged, but expanded.

As musicians and students, we understand that studying both classical music and jazz allows us to hone our musical skills. Similarly, the concepts specific to country blues provide the basis for a wide variety of playing styles from the early country traditions to jazz and contemporary music. Country blues is an art form defined by a precise craft. Just as we study the music of the jazz "greats" to develop our skills, learning the techniques of the original blues masters is a curriculum for musical inspiration and creativity.

It is also satisfying that many of Steve Calt's ideas that were important in my development as a musician have found some form of wider acceptance. Steve understood the fundamentals – about how the great blues and ragtime musicians managed to master their instruments and become great artists by treating the music as a craft and an art form.

Full Circle – "Harlem Street Singer"

Reverend Gary Davis has come back into my life decades after my final lesson with him. For the last 5 years, I co-produced a documentary about my former teacher, mentor, and guide called "Harlem Street Singer" with Trevor Laurence who also co-directed the film along with Simeon Hutner. This project was intended to tell the Rev. Gary Davis story and to show how he was one of the most important blues and ragtime musicians of the twentieth century. The film is our tribute to Davis' musical achievements and also an acknowledgment of his influence on the lives of those who were fortunate enough to have come into contact with this remarkable man. Funding for the film came from many supporters but it was Robert and Eileen who believed in the project from the outset, and, as executive producers, made it a reality.

The seeds of the Harlem Street Singer project were sewn a few years beforehand when I was hired to give guitar lessons to Sean Puffy Combs (aka "Puff Daddy" and "P. Diddy"). He was preparing to make a film based on the life and music of the great blues artist Robert Johnson. Evidently it was a real Hollywood production and a big deal. I did not see the script when we started and Sean did not play guitar, so it was just basic lessons from the beginning. It seemed very superficial from the outset; neither Sean nor the director talked to me about any aspects about country blues, the history or the musical styles. The lessons fizzled out and when I called the Director (or his office – I can't remember which) and was told that the project lost it's funding and that our guitar lessons intimidated Sean! I was not sure how to take that – this was a first for me. I think he was just out of his element. If the film were to be completed, the story of the blues and what little we know about Robert Johnson would be just a Hollywood drama. It made me realize that how some of the folklore around blues music, much of it fiction possibly, becomes history.
Around the same time Trevor and I were talking about making a film about Rev. Gary Davis. Trevor started writing up a draft proposal for the film and a brief story line. I had my tapes from my lessons

with Davis and I was involved with the musicians who knew Davis. It was the perfect "in-house" project for us to work on together. Davis was generally overlooked and never really got his due with the blues historians, so there seemed to be a story there that was begging to be told. And needed to be told.

The idea was not to just place him as part of a folk movement or a blues revival. Taking that approach is why he's a footnote in the history books. People don't know what to make of him because he did not fit into one category. He was not a jazz player, not a straight-ahead blues player, folk player, gospel or ragtime Player. I mean, *nobody* played like him. So he was easy for scholars to avoid by saying, "Oh he doesn't represent a tradition so we're not going to really talk about him."

Now more than ever, while there is still was an oral history to tell, we both felt it was an important project to do and the right time to do it - not only in terms of adding to Rev. Davis' legacy, but to document and spotlight his artistry and influence. One of the beautiful things about making the movie *Harlem Street Singer* was the opportunity to look at Davis for who he was.

Revisiting Rev. Davis' music after all these years has been fun, and at times frustrating. It has been a revealing experience looking back at my music and what it means to me. First, I realized once again just how great Davis was; hearing that sound, that togetherness and his solid rhythm hit me hard. Second, trying to re-learn his tunes was difficult. But through doing that, I understood more of what he was doing. I really listened to his repertoire from 1935 to 1971 and could hear even more clearly how his arrangements were worked out years ago, but how he also improvised within the song. Third, I realized that I had my own way of playing, phrasing, touch, feel etc. That, although with a lot of work and effort I could probably play and sound just like Davis, what was the point? I started to play his tunes my way – to interpret rather than merely copy them. It was all his in the center, but each time I revisited one of Davis' tunes, I worked through it in my way. Now when I play my interpretations of Davis' songs, it feels like a duet between the two of us.

I think about sitting in Davis' living room and hearing him say, "You can go out and play. Play what you know and it's all quiet." So Davis is always there, in the background.

When I think about it, I never had many gigs where I played Davis' songs. I didn't start with an early career of Davis songs that I carried on with. Commercially, it probably would have been a good move, building an audience over the years. I don't really know why – I just got into other things. I mean, when I eventually came back to the "acoustic" scene, performing solo concerts and recording CDs, people would come up to me and say, "I have your book, *Six Early Blues Guitarists*,[47] where have you been the last 15 years? I thought you were dead!" Of course, I hadn't moved anywhere – I was just playing jazz in New York instead.

In One Word...

The common theme between all my lessons, whether they were taken in Davis' front room, Lennie's house, or in Paredes' apartment, was honesty. It was about being honest as a person, being honest with myself. That is the 'final message.' It is not just about playing, but doing it in a certain way – with integrity and with respect. That is what Davis and Lennie taught me above all else. In fact I have always consciously tried to base my reputation in the music industry on honesty. One thing that has revealed itself to me over and over is that my work has been guided by my personal relationships. Over the years I have established long term friendships with people I met through work – festival promoters, club owners, publishers, and record company folks.

It seems to come back to authenticity. It is about who you are as a person and why you are making music. Ultimately every musician has to find their own way through the maze – to work out his or her own way of dealing with people. My approach works for me, although it has not always been an easy path. Once again I am reminded of another of Lennie's insights: *"the hardest thing about being an artist is surviving..."*

Chapter 8

And So Play On...

Tuesday, June 3, 2014. I find myself riding in a black London taxi, weaving its way through unfamiliar backstreets from where I am staying just off Sloane Square to the BBC studios near Oxford Circus, central London. Later that evening I am due to be interviewed by Paul Jones, a one-time member of the 1960's British pop band Manfred Mann (again, no relation to the founder of that band) who now presents a regular R&B music show on BBC Radio 2. I have met Paul on several occasions, each interview digging further into my music. He is someone who I think is very respectful of blues, ragtime, and classic rock 'n roll: basically all forms of American music. Importantly, I think he is also a supporter of the musicians and recognizes the effort and dedication that musicians put into trying to master their art. Each time that we speak, even if it is just to fill a 20 minute slot on his radio show, something new is revealed to me. A new question, a different angle on the music, hearing another person's perspective – it forces me to think about music in new ways. It helps me to discover new connections between my mentors and their music. In a sense the connection between these people is a result of musicians such as myself discovering their music and bringing their ideas into dialogue with each other. In my June 3rd interview with Paul, we talked about how master blues and jazz musicians approaches to improvising is not dissimilar. It is the ability to re-invent what they have already written that makes their music compelling – this is what validates the re-recordings of old tunes – so it always sounds like they just wrote them on the spot.

The interview also caused me to think about the past, about what my lessons with my mentors meant at the time, and now, decades, later. When I was with these guys – Davis, Lennie, Paredes – the world made sense to me. It is as if they managed to carve out their own worlds, their own aesthetic, and their own sensibility. Each of them managed to communicate a truth. It was not always an easy path that they chose to travel, but to me, they were right. The lessons I have learned from all of them are still relevant and inform whatever I am doing today, whether it's playing music, making a new CD or developing my teaching website. My past lessons translate into the present because their message was, at least to me, universal. Their 'truths' were often simple, but took courage. What matters is what they accomplished. Their work speaks for itself – no explanation is really necessary.

Great art just jumps out and grabs you. Time seems to stop and it feels like the only thing in life at that moment. There is no room for noise when you are in the moment – whether you are the receiver or the creator. For me, playing in front of an audience or simply practicing in the stairwell in my apartment building – gives me those moments.

NOTES

[1] Werner, Kenny. *Effortless Mastery: Liberating the Master Musician Within* (New Albany: Jamey Aebersold Jazz, 1996), p.99.

[2] Lightning Hopkins was born Sam John Hopkins in Centreville, Texas in 1912. As a young musician he was greatly influenced by Blind Lemon Jefferson, with whom he performed at church gatherings. He later developed a distinctive guitar style which incorporated both monotonic and alternating bass lines with rhythm parts and melody lines, all played simultaneously. Although he played almost exclusively in Texas during the 1940s and the 1950s, he reached a wider audience after he was discovered by Mack McCormick in 1959. He went on to record hundreds of songs and to perform regularly at folk festivals, folk clubs and university campuses before his death in 1982 aged 69.

[3] One of the most famous figures in blues history, Broonzy was born William Lee Conley Broonzy in Mississippi in 1898. He was raised in Pine Bluff, Arkanas. He took up the violin in childhood and is thought to have learned the guitar in the 1920s after moving to Chicago. Broonzy's recording career began in 1927, although he did not become commercially successful until the 1930s. His appearance at the 1938 "Spirituals to Swing' concert at Carnegie Hall brought him to the attention of white audiences. As his recording career declined in the late 1940s he discarded the electric guitar and assumed a new identity as a self-accompanied "folk" musician. By the time of his death in 1957 he had achieved considerable popularity in Europe, where he toured several times.

[4] *Big Bill Blues,* published in 1955, was the first autobiography by a blues artist.

[5] In very brief, Davis was born on 30 April 1896 in South Carolina. He was raised by his grandmother following the death of his father at an early age. Initially a street musician, he played blues, ragtime

and popular music of the day. In 1937 he was ordained as a Baptist minister after which his repertoire became focused on gospel music. Davis migrated to New York in the 1940s where he remained after his re-discovery during the 1960s. He died on 5 May, 1972. For a complete account of Davis' life try Robert Tilling's *Oh, What a Beautiful City! A Tribute to Rev. Gary Davis* (Jersey, Channel Islands: Paul Mill Press, 1992).

[6] Although he was one of the most skillful guitarists of his generation, Blake remains a historically obscure figure. Virtually nothing is known of him beyond the fact that he hailed from Jacksonville, Florida and born Arthur Blake. He first recorded for Paramount Records in 1926, eventually issuing 79 sides including blues, "rag-tunes" and instrumentals. He faded into obscurity during the Great Depression and is said to have died in the early 1930s.

[7] Like Blake, almost nothing is known about Bo Weavil Jackson, although it is believed that his real name was James Butler and was born in Birmingham Alabama. He was one of the first bluesmen to be recorded, in 1926, with sides issued on the Paramount and Vocalion labels.

[8] George "Little Hat" Jones was born in 1899 in Bowie County, Texas. A street musician during the 1920s, his entire recorded musical output was captured in just three recording dates for Okeh Records between 1929 and 1930. He never recorded again and died in 1981 in Texas.

[9] Although James had only a small reputation among his peers of the 1920s, he is regarded as one of the greatest blues artists of all time. Born Nehemiah James in 1902, he was raised in Bentonia, a hill country town south of the Mississippi Delta. He learned the guitar in childhood and first played professionally in around 1918 when he worked as a pianist in Weona, Arkanas. Soon afterwards he discovered the open E minor tuning in which he cast most of his guitar pieces. His single session in 1931 for Paramount Records resulted in

18 issued sides, and established him as the only bluesman of the period to excel on both guitar and piano. In late 1931 he started studying for the ministry, and made only sporadic forays into secular music until his rediscovery in 1964 in Tunica, Mississippi, when he was resurrected as a blues artist. He died in 1969 while living in Philadelphia.

[10] Born into a family of freed slaves in 1874, Henry Thomas was an itinerant songster and musician whose guitar style has come to be identified as the Texas blues guitar. He recorded 23 sides for the Vocalion label between 1927 and 1929, but nothing is known of his whereabouts after his final recording session in 1929.

[11] A peerless vocalist and unique musician, Jefferson stood only second to Bessie Smith as the most commercially appealing blues artist of the 1920s, yet few concrete details are known about his career. He was raised in Wortham, Texas, a small town sixty miles south of Dallas, and he traveled widely as an itinerant street singer. His hugely successful recording debut in 1926 sparked the vogue for self-accompanied blues singers. In the late 1920s he spent time in both Dallas and in Chicago, and he is said to have died in Chicago in 1929.

[12] A truly inspired guitarist and performer, Charlie Patton was Mississippi's first blues celebrity. Born in 1891, he was raised on the Delta plantation of Dockery and took up the guitar in around 1907. By the time he recorded for Paramount in 1929 he was long established as the state's leading blues dance entertainer. He died in 1934, three months after his last recording session.

[13] Bo Carter was one of the most inventive bluesmen of the 1930s. Born Armenter Chatmon in 1893, he originally worked with six musical brothers who formed a square-dance string band in their native Bolton, a hill country town in central Mississippi. In this capacity he played tenor banjo. His career as a solo guitarist dates back to the early 1930s when blindness caused him to work as a street musician. He recorded 106 sides between 1930 and 1940, mostly self-accompanied on his National guitar. Chatmon died in 1964.

[14] Mann, Woody. *The Anthology of Blues Guitar,* (Oak Publications: 1993), p.24. See also the musical examples at pp.25-27, which are intended to illustrate this idea.

[15] The Anthology of Blues Guitar, p.28.

[16] Alan Lomax held this post from 1937 to 1942 – See Wikipedia "Alan Lomax" accessed 21 April 2014.

[17] Calt, Stephen. *I'd Rather be the Devil* (Da Capo Press, 1995), p.220.

[18] ibid at p.219. This was also recognized by Paul Oliver in his 1965 book Conversations with the Blues, p.11.

[19] Lipscomb was born in 1895 and began playing the guitar, around 1909. He worked as a sharecropper, playing for weekend dances primarily around his hometown of Navasota, Texas, which numbered 5,100 people in 1930. Following his discovery in the 1960s he recorded numerous albums and appeared regularly on the concert circuit before dying in 1976.

[20] An unsurpassed slide guitarist, Blind Willie Johnson is thought to have been born in 1900 in Marlin, Texas, a town of 4,300 people in 1920. He moved to Dallas in the late 1920s, where he was first recorded in 1927. Between 1927 and 1930 he recorded some thirty sides, half of them vocal duets with his wife. By 1928 he had settled in Beaumont, Texas where he was still performing at the time of his death in the 1940s.

[21] One of the most popular blues recording artists of the 1930s, Fuller was born Fulton Allen in 1908 in Wadesboro, North Carolina. He began playing in the mid-1920s and became a professional street singer after losing his sight in the late 1920s. In the early 1930s he settled in Durham, North Carolina, where he learned guitar pointers from Rev. Gary Davis whom he met in 1935. Fuller made his first recordings that year, enjoying immediate commercial

success. He made a further 135 sides over the next five years before his death in 1941.

[22] A little known but locally dominant blues musician, Walker was born in 1896 in South Carolina. By 1910 he was living in Greenville, South Carolina, and was working in a string band with Rev. Gary Davis. His two surviving sides were recorded at a single 1930 session in tandem with a backing guitarist Sam Brooks. Having recorded a fraction of his repertoire, Walker died in 1933.

[23] Preface to "The Anthology of Blues Guitar" (1993) pp.8-9.

[24] Son House was a contemporary of Robert Johnson, the most storied figure in Blues music. House was born Eddie James House in 1902 in Lyon, Mississippi near Clarksdale. His recording career began in 1930 at a session with Paramount Records. He moved north to New York in 1942 shortly after being recorded by the Library of Congress. He was rediscovered in 1964 and survived until 1988.

[25] These recordings can be found on: Mann, Woody, Jo-Ann Kelly & Son House, Been Here and Gone (Catfish Records, 2003).

[26] Werner, Kenny. *Effortless Mastery* (New Albany: Jamey Aebersold Jazz, 1996), p.42.

[27] For a more complete biography of Lennie's life, read Enumi Shim's *Lennie Tristano; His Life in Music.*

[28] This is also the title of Stafford Chamberlain's biography of Marsh, An Unsung Cat: The Life and Music of Warne Marsh (Scarecrow Press, 2000). An appropriate title.

[29] D'Aquisto, James L., "An Interview with James D'Aquisto" in *Guitarmaker* (the magazine of The Association of Stringed Instrument Artisans (ASIA)) – interview in 3 parts: No.9 (October 1990); No.10 (December 1990); No.12 (June 1991).

[30] Attila received this award in 1964 and again in 1973.

[31] All of these tunes can be found on Attila's last record, Lasting Love (Acoustic Music Records, 1997).

[32] *The Birds and the Bees* was recorded with Herbie Hancock on Attila's record Gypsy Cry (Embryo Records, 1969).

[33] I first recorded this tune on my CD Stories (Flying Fish Records, 1993).

[34] Shim, Eunmi, *Lennie Tristano: His Life in Music* (University of Michigan Press, 2005), p.302.

[35] For a fuller account of the history of the Portuguese guitar, I would start with Professor Pedro Caldeira Cabral's *The Portuguese Guitar* (Ediclube: Lisbon, 1999). Prof. Cabral is recognized as a leading authority on the history of the instrument.

[36] The title to one of Carlos Paredes recordings – Paredes, Carlos. *Espelho de Sons* (EMI, 1987)

[37] Carlos Paredes – see the liner notes to *Espelho de Sons*.

[38] The Mondego is the river that runs through Paredes' hometown of Coimbra.

[39] Listen to the variations recorded on *Espelho de Sons* and on *Asas Sobre du Monde* (see Discography for details).

[40] Armandhino (born Amando Augusto Freire) was a highly influential guitarist from Lisbon. He was born in 1891 and died in 1946. He is a legendary figure in Portugal, as a Fado musician and composer.

[41] Discussion of T'ai Chi, flow and happiness and mastering life by Dr. Stewart McFarlane in "T'ai Chi Ch'uan. Wisdom in Action in a

Chinese Martial Art" (Mowbray Publishing: 2011), pp.62-67. E-pub at www.taichi-exercises.com

[42] Werner, Kenny. *Effortless Mastery* (New Albany: Jamey Aebersold Jazz, 1996), p.106.

[43] Werner, Kenny. *Effortless Mastery* (New Albany: Jamey Aebersold Jazz, 1996), p.59.

[44] Mann, Woody. *Six Early Blues Guitarists* (Music Sales Inc.: Oak Publications, 1973).

[45] Brendan McCormack was a performer with roots in the Mersey beat scene of the early 1960s – he was apparently one of John Lennon's favorite guitarists. He was also an accomplished classical guitarist who studied in Spain with Emilio Pujol, a former pupil of the composer Tarrega, and later founded the Liverpool Classical Guitar Society. Known as a great teacher, Brendan died of a heart attack in 2009.

Further Listening and Resources

Discography, Books and Teaching Materials

Recordings

Careless Love (solo) – Acoustic Sessions Recordings
Conversations (duo with Charley Krachy) – New Artist Records
Tribute to the Reverend (solo) – Acoustic Sessions Recordings
Empire Roots Band (with Dave Keyes, Bill Sims Jr., Brian Glassman)
  – Acoustic Sessions Recordings
Road Trip (solo) – Acoustic Sessions Recordings
Out of the Blue (with Susanne Vogt) – Acoustic Music Records
Waltz For Joy (with Susanne Vogt) – Acoustic Music Records
Together in Las Vegas (with John Cephas and Orville Johnson)
  – Acoustic Sessions Recordings
Been Here and Gone (with Son House and Jo Ann Kelly)
  – Catfish Records
Get Together (with Bob Brozman) – Acoustic Music Records
Heading Uptown (solo) – Shanachie Records
When I've Got the Moon (with Susanne Vogt)
  – Acoustic Sessions Recordings
Stairwell Serenade (solo) – Acoustic Music Records
Stories (solo) – Greenhays /Rounder Recordings
Old fashioned Love (with John Fahey) – Takoma Records

Books of Original Compositions

Stairwell Serenade (Acoustic Music Records)
Lisboa (Book with CD) (Music Sales Inc.)

Books

The Complete Blues Guitar Method (Music Sales Inc.)
Blues Roots (in English and German) (Acoustic Music Books)

Fingerstyle Guitar Workshop (in English and Italian)
Woody Mann & Davide Mastrangelo (Carish Publishing)
Bottleneck Blues Guitar (Music Sales Inc.)
The Gig Bag Book of Alternate Tunings (Music Sales Inc.)
The Blues Fakebook (Music Sales Inc.)
The Anthology of Blues Guitar (Music Sales Inc.)
The Complete Robert Johnson (Music Sales Inc.)
Six Early Blues Guitarists (Music Sales Inc.)

Teaching DVD's (Books & DVDs)

Take Command of your Fretboard (Homespun Tapes)
Art of Acoustic Blues Guitar – Handful of Riffs (Acoustic Sessions Inc.)
Art of Acoustic Blues Guitar – Do that Guitar Rag (Acoustic Sessions Inc.)
Art of Acoustic Blues Guitar – Early Roots (Acoustic Sessions Inc.)
Art of Acoustic Blues Guitar – The Basics (Music Sales Inc.)
Art of Acoustic Blues Guitar – The Logic of the Fretboard (Music Sales Inc.)
Art of Acoustic Blues – Ragtime and Gospel (Music Sales Inc.)
Masterpieces of Country Blues Guitar (Grossman's Guitar Workshop)
The Early Roots of Robert Johnson (Grossman's Guitar Workshop)
The Guitar of Robert Johnson (Grossman's Guitar Workshop)
The Guitar of Lonnie Johnson (Grossman's Guitar Workshop)
The Guitar of Blind Blake (Grossman's Guitar Workshop)
The Guitar of Big Bill Broonzy (Grossman's Guitar Workshop)
Country Blues Guitar Duets – with Bob Brozman (TAB Guitar School, Japan)
Delta Blues Guitar Duets – with Bob Brozman (TAB Guitar School, Japan)
Fingerstyle Blues Guitar (Grossman's Guitar Workshop)

Performance DVD's

Stairwell Serenade (Acoustic Music Records)
The Guitar Artistry of Woody Mann: Songs From The Blues
   (Grossman's Guitar Workshop)

Further Listening

Country Blues & Ragtime

The following list of 80 titles I compiled for a 4 CD set of country blues recordings for Acoustic Music Records, in Germany: *"The Essential Country Blues Guitar"* – Acoustic Music Records (319.2004.2).

It features the most important (and most recorded) artists as well as the obscure (but no less great) players who cut only a few sides. To me it represents the some of the most creative guitar arrangements and showcases a broad cross-section of styles from across the South. Here is the complete track listing for each of the volumes. You should be able to find most, if not all, of the titles online.

Volume One
1. Kokomo Blues, Scrapper Blackwell
2. Down the Dirty Road, Charlie Patton
3. Devil Got My Woman, Skip James
4. Mississippi Blues, Willie Brown
5. Away Down the Alley, Lonnie Johnson
6. Matchbox Blues, Blind Lemon Jefferson
7. Terraplane Blues, Robert Johnson
8. Little Leg Woman, Big Joe Williams
9. Future Blues, Willie Brown
10. Milk Cow Blues, Kokomo Arnold
11. Cairo Blues, Henry Spaulding
12. Gone Dead Train, King Soloman Hill
13. Dark Was the Night, Cold Was the Ground, Blind Willie Johnson
14. Screamin' and Hollerin' the Blues, Charlie Patton
15. Statesboro Blues, Blind Willie McTell
16. One Dime Blues, Blind Lemon Jefferson
17. Diddie Wa Diddie, Blind Blake
18. Candy Man, Mississippi John Hurt
19. Long Tall Mama, Big Bill Bronzy
20. South Carolina Rag, Willie Walker

Volume Two
1. Moon Going Down, Charlie Patton
2. Big Road Blues, Tommy Johnson
3. When You Got a Good Friend, Robert Johnson
4. Drunken Barrelhouse, Memphis Minnie
5. Bye Bye Baby Blues, Little Hat Jones
6. Crow Jane, Carl Martin
7. Tired of Being Mistreated, Clifford Gibson
8. To Do This You Got to Know How, Lonnie Johnson
9. Yo Yo Blues, Barbecue Bob
10. Bull Doze Blues, Henry Thomas
11. Keep It Clean, Charlie Jordan
12. Ragtime Millionaire, Willie Moore
13. Shave 'em Dry, Papa Charlie Jackson
14. Southern Rag , Blind Blake
15. I Belong to the Band, Rev. Gary Davis
16. Bull Cow Blues, Big Bill Broonzy
17. Special Agent, Sleepy John Estes
18. Hard Time Killing Floor, Skip James
19. Eagles On a Half, Geechie Wiley, John Byrd
20. Dry Spell Blues, Son House
21. You Can't Keep No Brown, Bo Weavil Jackson
22. Panama Limited, Bukka White

Volume Three
1. Pony Blues, Charlie Patton
2. Crossroad Blues, Robert Johnson
3. Playing With the Strings, Lonnie Johnson
4. Howling Wolf Blues, Funny Papa Smith
5. Lawdy Lawdy Worried Blues, Teddy Darby
6. Blind Arthur's Breakdown, Blind Blake
7. Boogie Woogie Dance, Tampa Red
8. Rising River Blues, George Carter
9. Motherless Child Blues, Barbecue Bob
10. Come On in My Kitchen, Robert Johnson
11. Special Rider Blues, Skip James

12. That's No Way to Get Along, Rev. Robert Wilkins
13. Roll and Tumble Blues, Hambone Willie Newburn
14. Don't Sell It, Don't Give It Away, Oscar Woods
15. Fishing Blues, Henry Thomas
16. Try Me One More Time, Marshal Owens
17. Fare Thee Well Blues, Joe Calicott
18. Preacher's Blues, Hi Henry Brown
19. No Woman No Nickle, Bumble Bee Slim
20. God Moves On the Water, Blind Willie Johnson

Volume Four
1. Stomping 'em Along Slow, Lonnie Johnson
2. I'm So Glad, Skip James
3. Blue Day Blues, Scrapper Blackwell
4. Catfish Blues, Robert Petway
5. Green River Blues, Charlie Patton
6. Rolling Log Blues, Lottie Kimbrough
7. Kindhearted Woman Blues, Robert Johnson
8. Mistreated Blues, Henry Townsend
9. Outside Woman Blues, Blind Joe Reynolds
10. I Believe I'll Dust My Broom, Robert Johnson
11. Good Boy Blues, Arthur Pettis
12. Turn You Money Green, Furry Lewis
13. Twelve Pound Daddy, Pearl Dickson, Pet and Can
14. Weeping Willow Blues, Blind Boy Fuller
15. Police Dog Blues, Blind Blake
16. The Law's Gonna Step On You, Bo Carter
17. Blues Gosse Blues, Jessie Thomas
18. Good Gal, Josh White
19. A Spoonful Blues, Charlie Patton
20. Brownskin Shuffle, Big Bill Broonzy

Here are some of my favorite albums – naturally many of them are on the Yazoo label. My list includes both anthologies and individual artist CDs – some artists didn't record enough sides to warrant an individual release, so picking up a few anthology collections is helpful to get full coverage of the Blues and Ragtime genres. These CDs offer each artist's greatest recordings.

Charlie Patton – *King of the Delta Blues* (Yazoo 2001)
Charlie Patton – *Founder of the Delta Blues* (Yazoo 2010)
Blind Boy Fuller – *Truckin' my Blues Away* (Yazoo 1060)
Blind Lemon Jefferson – *King of the Country Blues* (Yazoo 1069)
Blind Blake – *Ragtime Guitars' Foremost Fingerpicker* (Yazoo 1968)
Big Bill Broonzy – *The Young Big Bill Broonzy* (Yazoo 1011)
Skip James – *Complete Early Recordings* (Yazoo 2009)
Blind Willie McTell – *1927-1933 The Early Years* (Yazoo 1005)
Mississippi John Hurt – *1928 Sessions* (Yazoo 1065)
Scrapper Blackwell – *The Virtuoso Guitar of Scrapper Blackwell* (Yazoo 1019)
Blind Willie Johnson – *Praise God I'm Satisfied* (Yazoo 1058)
Tampa Red – *Bottleneck Guitar 1928-1937* (Yazoo 1039)
Reverend Gary Davis – *The Complete Early Recordings of
    Reverend Gary Davis* (Yazoo 2011)
Reverend Gary Davis – *Blues and Ragtime* (Shanachie 97024)
Robert Johnson – *The Complete Recordings* (Columbia)
Son House – *The Complete Library of Congress Sessions 1941-1942*
    (Travelin' Man TM CD 02)
Snooks Eaglin – *New Orleans Street Singer* (Storyville STCD 8023)
Various Artists – *East Coast Blues 1926-1935* (Yazoo 1013)
Various Artists – *Country Blues Bottleneck Guitar Classics* (Yazoo 1026)

Reverend Gary Davis

Feature documentary film "Harlem Street Singer", the story of Rev. Gary Davis. *Directed by Trevor Laurence and Simeon Hutner/Produced by Woody Mann and Trevor Laurence. www.harlemstreetsinger.com*

CDs: here are a few of my favorite Davis classics:

Davis, Revered Gary. *The Complete Early Recordings of Reverend Gary Davis* (Yazoo 2011)
Davis, Reverend Gary. *Harlem Street Singer* (Original Blues Classics)
Davis, Reverend Gary. *If I Had My Way* (Smithsonian Folkways)
Davis, Reverend Gary. *The Guitar and Banjo of Reverend Gary Davis* (Folklore Records)

Son House

Son House – *The Complete Library of Congress Sessions 1941-1942* (Travelin' Man TM CD 02)

His classic recordings from 1928-1930 have been issued on a number of anthologies including: *The Complete Recorded Works of Son House & the Great Delta Blues Singers* (Document Records)

The recording I made with Son House during the 1970s spotlights the power of his vocal performances, even in older age:

Been Here and Gone (with Son House and Jo Ann Kelly) (Acoustic Music Records 2003)

Lennie Tristano

Lennie was not a prolific recording artist. As a result, almost everything he released is required *listening*.

Tristano, Lennie. *Lennie Tristano* (Atlantic: 1955) – solo piano studio tracks and live tracks recorded with Lennie's great group from that era, with Lee Konitz, Warne Marsh, Arnold Fishkin, Peter Ind and Al Levitt. It includes a number of Lennie's classic lines, such as *Line Up* and *East 32nd Street*. For a glimpse of Lennie's prowess as an early innovator in studio recording techniques, try the cut *Turkish Mambo* (which is neither Turkish nor a Mambo).

Tristano, Lennie. *The New Tristano* (Atlantic: 1965) – solo piano improvisations. Be sure to let me know if you hear any solo piano improvisations which surpass Lennie's *C Minor Complex*.

Tristano, Lennie. *Intuition* (Proper Records Ltd – Properbox 64) A 4 CD box set. This includes Lennie's group sessions, including *Intuition and Digression*.

Lennie Tristano Quartet. *Live at the Confucius Restaurant 1955* (Gambit Records). A double CD containing live recordings of one of Lennie's classic groups, together with a few bonus tracks taken from his 1955 album, *Lennie Tristano*.

Tristano, Lennie. *The Copenhagen Concert* (1965). This is a DVD release of original film footage of Lennie performing solo in a concert setting. The footage is in black and white.

Warne Marsh

Some of Warne's greatest recordings are difficult to find and in some cases appear to be in and out of print. "The Art of Improvisation", originally released on Wave Records, is, to me, one of his greatest recordings. Here are a few, which should be available more readily. (But you can't go wrong with any of Warne's CDs).

Lee Konitz, with Warne Marsh (Atlantic 8122-75356-2: 1955). This contains Lee and Warne's treatment of a number of classic tunes from the standard repertoire, including: *I Can't Get Started, There Will Never Be Another You and Donna Lee.*

"Jazz of Two Cities" (Blue Note reissue series 147366)

Attila Zoller

Attila has a significant recorded back catalog as a solo artist, a collaborator and as a sideman.

His solo work is captured on his last recording
Zoller, Attila. *Lasting Love* (Acoustic Music Records: 1997)

As a band leader, a couple of high points include the following recordings:

Zoller, Attila. *Common Cause* (Enja Records: re-released 2009).
A classic trio recording with Ron Carter and Joe Chambers.

Zoller, Attila. *When It's Time* (Enja Records ENJ-9031 2: 1995). A late quartet recording with Lee Konitz, Larry Willis, Santi Debriano and Yoron Israel, containing a mixture of standard tunes and Attila's own compositions.

Attila was particularly proud of his duo recording with Jimmy Raney:
Zoller, Attila & Jimmy Raney. *Jim & I* (L&R Records: 1980).

Carlos Paredes

Carlos Paredes recordings are consistent. They are all great. What I find fascinating about his recordings is the way he re-records many of his tunes with different arrangements, additional sections (and sometimes different titles). There is so much to learn in his approach to composition, arranging and improvisation. Here are my favorites.

Paredes, Carlos. *Guitarra Portugesa*
   (EMI 0777 7 48674 2 9: 1967)
Paredes, Carlos. *Movimento Perpetuo*
   (Som Livre/EVC VSL 1214-2: 1971)
Paredes, Carlos. *Espelho de Sons*
   (Philips/PolyGram Portugal 934 319-2: 1987)
Paredes, Carlos. *Assas de Mondo*
   (Philips/PolyGram Portugal 842 412-2: 1989)

www.ingramcontent.com/pod-product-compliance
Lightning Source LLC
Chambersburg PA
CBHW071512040426
42444CB00008B/1602